TABLE OF CONTENTS

MW00885424

INSTRUCTIONS

WHAT IS A DOODLE?

For the sake of this scripture journal, a doodle is any drawing, words, diagrams, etc. that come to your mind as you are studying. This journal is a place for you to study the Book of Mormon and fill it with anything that helps you learn, understand, and record!

With a doodle journal, you can be as creative as you want as you study. Everyone's journal should be different!

For example, see the excerpts below that all come from this scripture journal. See how different they can be!

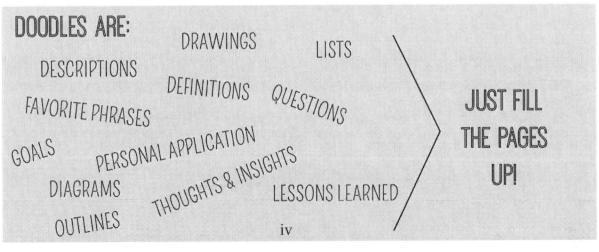

DOODLES ARE:

DESCRIPTIONS DRAWINGS LISTS
DEFINITIONS QUESTIONS
FAVORITE PHRASES
GOALS PERSONAL APPLICATION
DIAGRAMS THOUGHTS & INSIGHTS LESSONS LEARNED
OUTLINES

JUST FILL THE PAGES UP!

JERUSALEM ⊙ LEHI'S DAY

Open up to your Bible Maps and find Bible Map #9: "The World of the Old Testament". On that map find "Jerusalem," "Egypt," and "Babylon". Write those three places on the map below in their proper location.

Below is an illustration that explains the story of Jerusalem in Lehi's day. Read the story before you study 1 Nephi 1. You can color, add pictures, doodle thoughts, etc.

Babylona was going to destroyed Jerusalem

During Lehi's days in Jerusalem, the Pharaoh of Egypt had political control over the Kingdom of Judah (the Jews). They were allowed to live in their homeland but were still captive to Egypt.

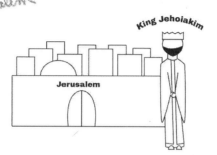

Although the Jews were not free, they had their own Jewish king. That king just did whatever the Pharaoh wanted him to do. Their king at the time was King Jehoiakim.

In 605 B.C. there was a battle that caused Babylon to win control over the Kingdom of Judah. The Babylonian King (King Nebuchadnezzar) now had control over the Kingdom of Judah.

King Jehoiakim remained the king of the Jews, but would now answer to Babylon instead of Egypt. However, it wasn't long until he revolted against Babylon.

King Nebuchadnezzar responded to the revolt by sending his army to Jerusalem and they took over the city.

Jehoiachin (Jehoiakim's son) took over the throne as king and surrendered to Babylon. With so much political turmoil, Jerusalem was in a fragile state.

After Jehoiachin, Nebuchadnezzar appointed 21-year-old Zedekiah to the throne. He was the uncle of Jehoiachin. Also, at this time, Jerusalem was full of wickedness.

Zedekiah chose to seek an alliance with Egypt to break free from Babylon.

Jeremiah, who was the prophet at the time, warned the people that if they did not repent their city would be destroyed and the people would be led into captivity.

2N4:34,35,

1 NEPHI 1 _____

Verses 1-3

Doodle what you learn about Nephi and the record he is making

Verse 4

Doodle what you learn about Lehi in this verse

Verses 5-7

Doodle what happened to Lehi

Verses 8-14

Doodle the vision Lehi has

Verses 15-17

Pick an important phrase in these verses and doodle it here. Include why you chose it out of all of the other phrases.

Verses 18-20

Doodle what happened to Lehi

1 NEPHI 2

1 Nephi 2:1-2

Doodle what is happening in verses 1 and 2 here: ➘

Consider the choice Lehi had to make. Consider the consequences to each choice below. Write what the consequences would or could be for each choice.

To obey and depart into the wilderness with his family

To stay in Jerusalem with his family.

1 Nephi 2:3-11

Study verses 3-11. Doodle on this picture things you learn. You can add pictures, questions, insights, descriptions, etc.

over 600 miles

Red Sea

1 Nephi 2:12-24

What do you learn about these five people in these verses? Doodle what you learn under each name and picture.

Lehi

Laman and Lemuel

Nephi

Sam

1 NEPHI 3-4 _____

Study 1 Nephi 3 -4 and fill this map in with details by doodling more pictures, people, words and descriptions.

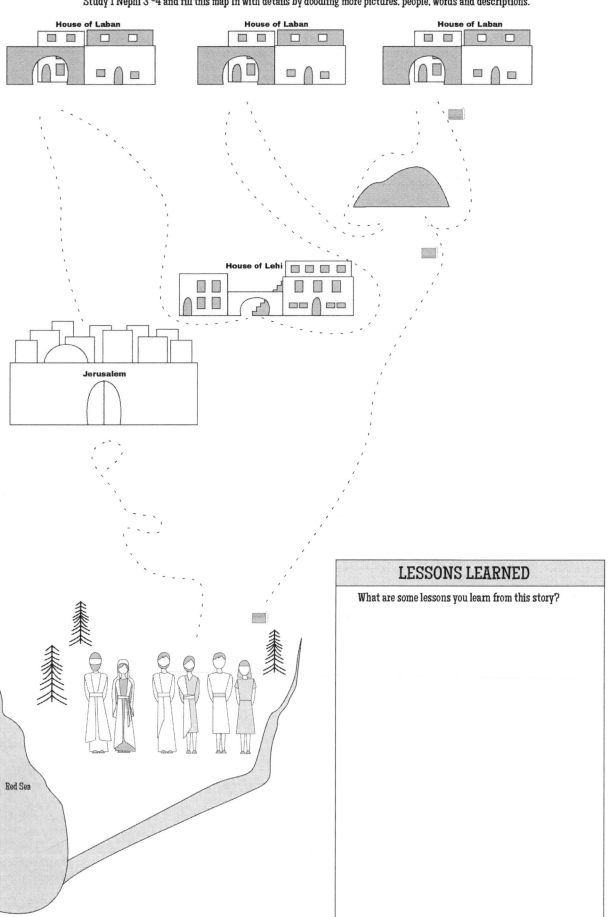

House of Laban

House of Laban

House of Laban

House of Lehi

Jerusalem

Red Sea

LESSONS LEARNED

What are some lessons you learn from this story?

1 NEPHI 5-6

1 Nephi 5:1-10

Study the interactions between Lehi and his wife Sariah. Doodle ALL of the principles you can find in this conversation. Specifically look for characteristics between a righteous husband and wife and how they depend upon one another.

1 Nephi 5:11-22

Doodle everything you learn about the plates of brass in these verses.

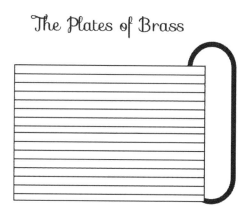

The Plates of Brass

1 Nephi 6:1-6

Doodle 4 important things that you learn in this chapter.

❶

❷

❸

❹

1 NEPHI 7

_____

Title for this chapter

Study all of 1 Nephi 7 and fill this map in with details by doodling more pictures, people, words and descriptions. Include principles and phrases you like as well.

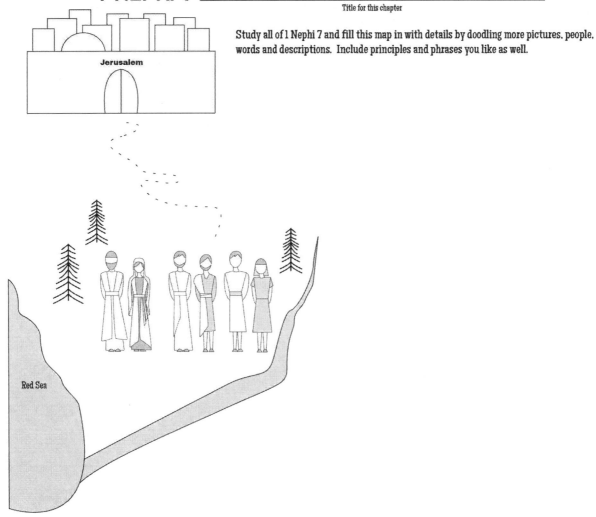

Jerusalem

Red Sea

Look at Nephi's words to those that were rebelling (verses 8-15). Doodle some of your favorite things he said.

What are all of the lessons you can learn from Nephi in this chapter?

13

1 NEPHI 8

Study 1 Nephi 8 about Lehi's vision. This illustration gives you a start of the vision. Study the chapter and add pictures, descriptions, labels and your own thoughts.

Be sure to include the 6 types of people Lehi saw on the strait and narrow path in his vision:

First group (verses 21-23)
Second group (verses 24-25)
Third group (verse 30)
Fourth group (verse 31)
Fifth group (verse 32)
Sixth group (verse 32)

The House of Israel is a major theme throughout the Book of Mormon. Lets take a minute and review what it is.

ABRAHAM

Abraham was a great prophet who made a covenant with god called "The Abrahamic Covenant"

THE ABRAHAMIC COVENANT

This was a very important covenant. The Abrahamic Covenant includes all Gospel covenants, and thus promised Abraham the ability to gain eternal life. In return, Abraham promised to bear the Priesthood and teach the Gospel to the rest of God's children

Abraham's Family

Abraham was promised that this covenant would be renewed with all of his posterity. So they would all have the covenants of eternal life, and the responsibility to teach the rest of God's children.

This is Abraham's Family

| Reuben | Simeon | Levi | Judah | Dan | Naphtali |
| Gad | Asher | Issachar | Zebulun | Joseph | Benjamin |

| Abraham | Isaac | Jacob |

Abraham had a son named Isaac. He had other sons, too, but Isaac was the "birthright" son and was the next prophet.

Isaac had a son named Jacob.

Jacob's name was changed to ISRAEL. Israel had 12 sons.

Some of the names for this family are:
THE HOUSE OF ISRAEL
THE CHILDREN OF ISRAEL
ISRAELITES

The below explanations can help you understand the House of Israel and what has happened to them (us) over the years. As you study, doodle your thoughts and questions all over the page and map.

For generations after, all Israelites knew from which of the 12 sons they descended. Each son had his own "tribe" made up of his descendants. So one may have been of the "Tribe of Judah" and another the "Tribe of Asher".

Out of the 12 sons, Joseph was the "birthright" son, and so he stood at the head of his family. He had two sons: Ephraim and Manasseh. Joseph's descendants specifically identified themselves through his sons. So his descendants would be of the "Tribe of Ephraim" or the "Tribe of Manasseh".

The Land of Israel was divided and each tribe inherited a portion of the land. Jerusalem was the capital city and where the temple was.

Over time, the Israelites decided they wanted a king like the other nations had. The Prophet Samuel warned them against having a king because wicked kings would corrupt the people God had chosen to be examples to the rest of His children. However, the people decided they wanted a king anyway.

The Israelites had many kings over many generations. Some kings were righteous, and others were very wicked. Eventually, there arose a divide among the people and 10 tribes split from 2 of the tribes (Judah and Benjamin).

The 10 tribes will be known as the Northern Tribes or the "Kingdom of Israel" and they will have their own king. The other 2 tribes will be known as the "Southern Tribes" or the "Kingdom of Judah" (or the Jews) and will have their own king. The Kingdom of Judah will have the capital city of Jerusalem.

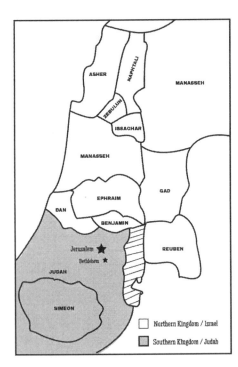

Northern Kingdom / Israel
Southern Kingdom / Judah

Over time, the Northern tribe became increasingly wicked until they no longer had God's protection. The Assyrians eventually capture them and carry many of them off to other nations. There, they will eventually become like those nations and worship as those nations worship. From thenceforth, they will be known as the "lost tribes of Israel" and are likened unto sheep who are lost and scattered from their flock. The Prophets will then write of a day when their people will be "gathered" back as descendants of Abraham and the covenant they are heirs to. In fact, the majority of the last part of the Bible is all about this, as well as the Book of Mormon.

This gathering has begun in these last days. Individuals are gathered, one at a time, as they are baptized. They will then, at some point, receive their Patriarchal Blessing which will declare which of the 12 tribes they have descended from.

At the beginning of the Book of Mormon, Lehi is living in Jerusalem and the Northern tribe has already been captured by Assyria; and now the Southern tribes are risking captivity by the Babylonians.

After Lehi departs, Babylon does capture the Kingdom of Judah and carries many off to Babylon (like Daniel, Shedrach, Meshach, and Abed-Nego). However, eventually Judah later returns to Israel and rebuilds their land. Christ was born after these events and during a time the Romans had power over Israel.

Put a sticky note here and label it "Explanation of The House of Israel". Now as you study and need a quick refresher, you can jump back to these pages easily.

LIKE AN OLIVE TREE...

Wild Tree

Branch of Healthy Tree

The House of Israel is often compared to an olive tree.

"Grafting" was a common practice in ancient times where you would take a branch from one tree and insert it into a different tree.

One purpose of doing this might be to help an olive tree which was no longer bearing fruit. One would take a branch from a healthy tree and "Graft" it into the wild tree in hopes that it would strengthen the tree.

Sometimes the House of Israel is compared to the branches that are grafted into the wild tree. Other times the House of Israel is compared to the wild tree that once bore fruit and the Lord is trying to strengthen again. And other times, the House of Israel is like a scattered or lost branch being inserted into the true tree.

WHAT IS A "GENTILE"?

The Book of Mormon often refers to "Gentiles," but what is a Gentile?

Look up "Gentile" in your Bible Dictionary. Write the first sentence of the defintion here:

Example:

Israelite   Gentile

What are the two common uses of the word Gentile (first paragraph in your Bible Dictionary under "Gentile")?

Circle which one of the two uses is commonly used in the Book of Mormon (explained in the last sentence of the first paragraph in your Bible Dictionary).

1 NEPHI 9-10 _____

1 NEPHI 9

Study 1 Nephi 9. Nephi teaches us about the two separate sets of plates he kept. Doodle around each set of plates things you learn about them. Use the chapter heading for clarity.

The Plates of Nephi

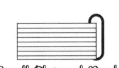

Small Plates of Nephi

Large Plates of Nephi

1 NEPHI 10

Verses 1-11

Doodle the things Lehi prophesies about

Verses 12-14

In these verses Lehi compares the House of Israel to an Olive Tree. Doodle about this here.

Verses 15-22

Nephi bears his testimony in these verses. Find your favorite phrase and doodle it here.

1 NEPHI 11: NEPHI'S VISION

Doodle what is happening and what you are learning in these groups of verses. Try to find important doctrines and principles and include them in your boxes.

11:1	**11:2-6**	**11:7-9**
11:10-11	**11:12-15**	**11:16-18**
11:19-20	**11:21-23**	**11:24-25**
11:26-29	**11:30**	**11:31**
11:32-33	**11:34-35**	**11:36**

1 NEPHI 12: NEPHI'S VISION _____

Doodle what is happening and what you are learning in these groups of verses. Try to find important doctrines and principles and include them in your boxes.

12:1	12:2-3	12:4
12:5-6	12:7-8	12:9-10
12:11-12	12:13-14	12:15
12:16	12:17	12:18
12:19	12:20-21	12:22-23

Title for this chapter

Doodle what is happening and what you are learning in these groups of verses. Try to find important doctrines and principles and include them in your boxes.

13:1-3	13:4-6	13:7-9
13:10-13	13:14-16	13:17-19
13:20-23	13:24-26	13:27-29
13:30-33	13:34	13:35-37
13:38-39	13:40-41	13:42

1 NEPHI 14: NEPHI'S VISION

Doodle what is happening and what you are learning in these groups of verses. Try to find important doctrines and principles and include them in your boxes.

14:1-4	14:5-6	14:7
14:8-10	14:11-13	14:14-15
14:16-17	14:18-20	14:21-22
14:23-26	14:27	14:28-30

_____

Title for this chapter

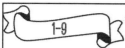

1-9   Study verses 1-9. FILL this box with principles and teachings you find in these verses.

Study verses 10-20 and explain this illustration below. Doodle all over this part of the page what you learn, your thoughts, questions, etc.

True Olive Tree

Gathering of scattered branches

Study verses 21-36 and add any insights you learned about Lehi's vision to your diagram on page 14.

Doodle some important doctrines and principles you learned from this chapter:

1 NEPHI 16 _____

Study verses 1-6 and fill this box with doctrines and principles you find.

Below is a timeline. Study verses 7-24 and, in order, fill the timeline with the events of those verses.

←——————————————————————————————→

The Liahona

Draw a picture of what you think the Liahona could have looked like. (use verse 10 for a description).	What are some specific things we learn about the Liahona from verses 25-26?

Continue the timeline above as you study verses 30-39

←——————————————————————————————→

What lessons do you learn from Nephi in this chapter?

1 NEPHI 17:1-22

Title for this chapter

Study verses 1-3 and fill this box with doctrines and principles you find.

In this space, doodle what was happening in verses 4-6.

NOW WHAT? Now that they have traveled as far as to a seashore, what now? What options do they have? Doodle your thoughts here:

In the left column, doodle what is happening in verses 7-16. In the right column, doodle your thoughts, insights and lessons learned in these verses.

WHAT IS HAPPENING	LESSONS LEARNED

Laman and Lemuel

Study verses 17-22. Look for statements that Laman and Lemuel made that were false and showed the state of their minds and hearts. Doodle those statements here. By your doodles of their statements, add your thoughts as to why their statements were wrong.

After reading verses 18-22, what advice would you give to Laman and Lemuel?

Nephi's response

Study verses 22-55. Doodle doctrines and principles Nephi said to his brothers in response to verses 18-22. Also doodle things Nephi did. After you have doodled about those verses, step back and look at everything you found and consider why those were good things for Nephi to say or do in that situation. Record your thoughts around each doodle.

1 NEPHI 18

Doodle about these verses in this chapter. You can include pictures, explanations, doctrines and principles taught, personal insights, questions, etc.

18:1	18:2-3	18:4
18:5-7	18:8-9	18:10-11
18:12-14	18:15-16	18:17-19
18:20-21	18:22-23	18:24-25

1 NEPHI 19

Study verses 1-5 and doodle what you learn about the plates of Nephi.

The Plates of Nephi

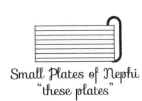

Small Plates of Nephi
"these plates"

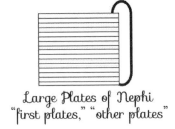

Large Plates of Nephi
"first plates," "other plates"

Study verses 6-18. Doodle things you find that fall into the following categories. Put a star next to prophecies taught by prophets that Nephi learned from.

Prophecies of Future Events	Teachings from the past

Doodle important teachings you find in verses 19-24.

1 NEPHI 20

Tip

In this chapter Nephi begins quoting prophecies from Isaiah that he had studied from the Brass plates. Isaiah is speaking to the Jews of his day and chastising them for claiming to follow the Lord while not keeping the commandments (verses 1 and 2).

FILL IN THE FOUR BOXES BELOW AS YOU STUDY THIS CHAPTER.

DEFINITIONS

As you study this chapter, look up words you do not understand. Doodle those words and their definitions in this box.

VERSE 2

STAY: TO STICK OR REMAIN WITH

IMAGERY

Isaiah uses a lot of imagery to help communicate truth. Imagery is visual or figurative (not literal) language. Whenever you come across some of his imagery, doodle it in this box, along with what you think that imagery represents.

VERSE: 4 "NECK IS AN IRON SINEW"
-IRON IS HARD AND UNBENDABLE.
-SINEW IS WHAT UNITES BONE TO MUSCLE
= THEIR NECKS WERE UNBENDABLE.
SPIRITUALLY, THEY WERE NOT HUMBLE
BEFORE GOD AND WOULD NOT BOW
BEFORE HIM IN HUMILITY.

UNFAITHFUL ISRAEL

Doodle words or phrases that indicate that Israel had not been faithful to the Lord and their covenants.

COVENANTS

NOT IN TRUTH & RIGHTEOUSNESS

VERSE 1

...OUT OF THE WATERS OF BAPTISM, WHO SWEAR BY THE NAME OF THE LORD, AND MAKE MENTION OF THE GOD OF ISRAEL, YET THEY SWEAR NOT IN TRUTH NOR IN RIGHTEOUSNESS.

MERCY FOR ISRAEL

Doodle words or phrases that show that the Lord is inviting Israel to return to Him.

1 NEPHI 21

Title for this chapter

Tip

In this chapter Nephi continues quoting Isaiah. In the last chapter Isaiah was speaking to the Jews of his day and in this chapter he emphasizes that Christ will not forget his covenant people.

DEFINITIONS

As you study this chapter, look up words you do not understand. Doodle those words and their definitions in this box.

ISRAEL IS NOT FORGOTTEN

Verses 1-21 reveal the Lord's love for His people. Doodle some phrases that you find in these verses that show you how much He loves Israel.

ISRAEL IN THE LAST DAYS

Verses 22-26 teaches that Israel will be gathered with power in the last days (see chapter heading). Doodle some things you learn about the gathering of Israel in the last days.

Tip

In this chapter Nephi wrote about the meaning of the last two chapters and how he explained them to his brothers.

Doodle about these verses in this chapter. You can include pictures, explanations, doctrines and principles taught, personal insights, questions, etc.

22:1	22:2-3	22:4-5
22:6-7	22:8-9	22:10-12
22:13-14	22:15-17	22:18-20
22:21-23	22:24-26	22:27-31

2 NEPHI 1

This chapter contains words of Lehi, who would shortly die. These are loving words of a parent pleading with them to obey the commandments of God. On this page, doodle 10 things he taught or said to them. Also, include why you think he would share that with them and why that teaching or saying may impact them.

1

2

3

4

5

6

7

8

9

10

2 NEPHI 2:1-14

This chapter is Lehi speaking to his son Jacob. In this chapter he teaches Jacob some really powerful doctrines. Doodle what you learn in each box. In some cases, finish the doodle already provided for you.

		LAW LAW: A SYSTEM OF ETERNAL RULES AND ORDER * this verse is referencing the consequences that occurred in the Garden of Eden TEMPORAL LAW SPIRITUAL LAW
2:1-3	**2:4**	**2:5**
BECAUSE OF THE LAW, WHAT DO WE NEED?		Firstfruits: This is an agricultural term referring to the first fruits or harvest of the season. Biblically, this refers to the first harvest (sacrifice or offering) given to God. Intercession: the act of intervening on behalf of another
2:6-7	**2:8**	**2:9**
	OPPOSITION WE CAN BE Righteous Wicked Holy Miserable Good Bad	**NO OPPOSITION** Righteous Wicked Bad Holy Miserable Good
2:10	**2:11-12**	
	THINGS TO ACT TO BE ACTED UPON	In the grand division of all of God's creations, there are things to act and things to be acted upon (see 2 Nephi 2:13-14). As sons and daughters of our Heavenly Father, we have been blessed with the gift of moral agency, the capacity for independent action and choice. Endowed with agency, you and I are agents, and we primarily are to act and not just be acted upon. To believe that someone or something can make us feel offended, angry, hurt, or bitter diminishes our moral agency and transforms us into objects to be acted upon. As agents, however, you and I have the power to act and to choose how we will respond to an offensive or hurtful situation. Elder David A. Bednar October 2006 General Conference
2:13	**2:14**	

2 NEPHI 2:15-30 _____

Title for this chapter

This chapter is Lehi speaking to his son Jacob. In this chapter he teaches Jacob some really powerful doctrines. Doodle what you learn in each box. In some cases, finish the doodle already provided for you.

Tree of Knowledge
of Good and Evil
(Forbidden Fruit)

Tree of Life

2:15-16

THE DEVIL

2:17-18

2:19-20

2:21

2:22-24

Adam's Role

Christ's Role

2:25

2:26

Our Role

2:27-30

33

_____

Title for this chapter

Tip

In this chapter Lehi is speaking to his son Joseph and tells him of their ancestor Joseph of Egypt, and also of a future Joseph who God has a great work for.

Study this chapter and doodle everything you learn about each of these Josephs. *Note: Joseph Smith, Sr. (Joseph Smith's father is mentioned once in verse 15).

JOSEPH
Lehi's Son

JOSEPH OF EGYPT

JOSEPH SMITH

2 NEPHI 4

LEHI TO THE CHILDREN OF LAMAN

Doodle what Lehi said to the children of Laman in verses 1-7

LEHI TO THE CHILDREN OF LEMUEL

Doodle what Lehi said to the children of Lemuel in verses 8-10

LEHI TO SAM

Doodle what Lehi said to Sam in verse 11

LEHI DIES

Doodle what happened in verses 12-14

NEPHI'S PSALM

Many people refer to verses 15-35 as "Nephi's Psalm". Doodle some of your favorite phrases from his psalm.

2 NEPHI 5

Doodle what is happening and principles you find in verses 1-5

Doodle everything you learn about the Nephites and the Lamanites in verses 6-28

NEPHITES
Verses 6-18, 26-28

LAMANITES
Verses 19-25

Doodle or record what is happening, and principles you find in verses 29-34

2 NEPHI 6 _____

Title for this chapter

Tip

In the last chapter Jacob was made a priest and a teacher over the people (2 Nephi 5:26). Chapters 6-10 are a record of his words as he fulfilled his responsibility and taught the Nephites.

Doodle what you learn and principles you find in verses 1-5

What message did Jacob want his people to understand when he quoted Isaiah? Doodle what you learn from Isaiah in verses 6-7

Record on this timeline what Jacob teaches his people about the Jews (House of Israel) who are in Jerusalem.

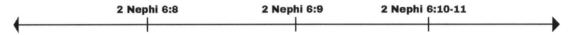

2 Nephi 6:8   **2 Nephi 6:9**   **2 Nephi 6:10-11**

Doodle important teachings you find in verses 8-18

2 NEPHI 7 _____

Tip

In this chapter Jacob is quoting Isaiah 50. Isaiah is writing as if he were Christ and is speaking to the Israelites who were scattered and in captivity to other nations because of their sins.

What does the Lord say in verse 1 to help the Israelites understand why they are separated from God?

_____

Doodle things that the Lord has done (or will do) for Israel in verses 2-9.

_____

Tip   Doodle what you learn about in verses 10 and 11 below. Be sure to include your own thoughts and insights.

Verse 10 is referring to believers who trust in the light of the Gospel rather than their own light. Verse 11 is referring to those who do not look to the Lord but rather make their own fire and provide their own light.

VERSE 10

VERSE 11

2 NEPHI 8 _____

Tip

In this chapter Jacob quotes Isaiah and his teachings about the gathering of scattered Israel in the latter-days.

Doodle the blessings that are promised to Israel as they are gathered as well as anything you find that shows the Lord's desire to redeem His people.(verses 1-16)

8:1-3	8:4-5	8:6-7	8:8
8:9-10	8:11-12	8:13-14	8:15-16

*Tip: In verse 9 Isaiah is referring to mythical enemies that are part of the sea. Rehab refers to storms which can wreak havoc and cause great destruction, as can the dragon which is a mythical sea serpent.

What are some of the above blessings you have experienced?

Study verses 17-25 and doodle prophecies you find about the gathering of Israel in the last days.

2 NEPHI 9

Tip

This chapter is still part of Jacob's teachings to the Nephites. He is no longer quoting Isaiah and will give a powerful sermon about the Atonement of Jesus Christ. Doodle important doctrines and principles you find in each verse. We have given you some titles for the boxes. Come up with your own titles for the boxes without titles.

	Our future resurrection	Christ will be resurrected
9:1-3	9:4	9:5
Power of resurrection	What would happen to our BODIES if there were no resurrection	What would happen to our SPIRITS if there were no resurrection
9:6	9:7	9:8-9
The Atonement delivers us from death of the body and the spirit	Temporal death (death of the body)	Spiritual death
9:10	9:11	9:12
The Resurrection	Judgment	
9:13-14	9:15-16	9:17-18

		9:25-26
9:19-21	9:22-24	
9:27	9:28	9:29-38
9:39	9:40	9:41
9:42-43	9:44-45	9:46-48
9:49-50	9:51-52	9:53-54

2 NEPHI 10

Verses 1-2
Doodle doctrines and principles you learn in these verses

Verses 3-5
Doodle what you learn about Christ and the Jews that live in His day

Verse 6
Doodle what you learn about the scattering of the Jews

Verses 7-9
Doodle what you learn about the gathering of the Jews in the last days

Verses 10-19
Doodle what you learn about the land of America

Verses 20-22
Doodle what you learn about others of the House of Israel (not just the Jews in Jerusalem)

Verses 23-25
Doodle the doctrines and principles you learn in these verses

2 NEPHI 11 _____
Title for this chapter

In this box, doodle the things in this chapter that Nephi's soul delights in	Doodle what you learn about Isaiah and his writings

Doodle some of your favorite phrases from this chapter	Doodle things that your soul delights in

Title for this chapter

For the next several chapters, Nephi quotes Isaiah. We have Isaiah in our Old Testament, Nephi had his words on the Brass Plates.

In these boxes, doodle what you learn in each set of verses. Write what is happening, draw pictures, make diagrams, write definitions, ask questions, record your insights, or record quotes from latter-day prophets that teach about similar issues in our day.

Verse 1

In Hebrew, "word" can also be translated as "message".

Verse 2

A mountain is symbolic of a high place where God comes to communicate with His people.

The term "when" suggests that the temple needed to be built in order for the events to follow.

Verse 3

These are events that will occur and/or precede the Millennium. Temples will cover the earth, but two great temples will be built. One in the New Jerusalem ("Zion") and the other in Old Jerusalem ("Jerusalem").

Verse 4

Notice that the rebuking in this verse causes positive change.

Verses 5-6

- House of Jacob = House of Israel
- One Hebrew translation for "forsaken" means to disperse or spread about.
- "Replenished from the east": Anciently, east was a sacred direction. These verses suggest they are looking to other sources for spiritual guidance.
- Another translation for "please themselves" is "clasp hands".

Verses 7-9

These verses describe the state of the people and their society.

Verses 10-12

These verses explain what the consequences will be for the people.

Verse 13

"Cedars of Lebanon" and "Oaks of Bashan" were both trees that produced highly valued wood used for fancy furniture and buildings.

Verses 14-15

Verse 16

The ships that Isaiah is referencing were commercial ships. The Ships of Tarshish were likely from a region in Spain, and these ships were known for being especially strong and able to withstand the forces of the sea.

Pleasant pictures were the statues or standards at the heads of the ships.

Verses 17-18

Verse 19

"To shake terribly the earth": This could literally mean that there will be a great earthquake, or it could mean that all of the values and prideful things of the world will come falling down.

Verses 20-21

"To the moles and to the bats": These are animals that cannot see and certainly would not value these items.

Verse 22

This verse emphasizes the frailty of man, of which the people are placing all of their trust. They are putting all of their faith in the hands of man, when he is always a breath away from death.

2 NEPHI 13

In this chapter, Nephi is quoting Isaiah. Isaiah is teaching about the consequences which will come upon the wicked.

In these boxes, doodle what you learn in each set of verses. Write what is happening, draw pictures, make diagrams, write definitions, ask questions, record your insights, or record quotes from latter-day prophets that teach about similar issues in our day.

Verse 1
"Stay and staff" means that the whole supply of bread and water will be taken away.

Verses 2-3
These verses are referring to men and women who aspire to high positions.

Verse 4
Rather than experienced leaders, young and inexperienced men will be placed in these leadership positions. The 7 kings following Isaiah's death (Manasseh, Amon, Josiah, Jehoahaz, Jehoiakim, Jehoiachin, and Zedekiah) all became kings between the ages of 8-25.

Verse 5
In such a state of wickedness and poor leadership, chaos ensues and there is a disrespect towards the older generations. There is also a state of oppression and competition among neighbors.

Verses 6-7
Brothers are looking for leadership in the family because the father has either died in war or abandoned his family.
They are not mentioning that they are taking hold of the older brother to rule the family but rather someone who at least has clothing. Each brother is refusing the role to lead.

Verses 8-9
The reasons that Jerusalem will be destroyed.

People cannot hide their sins. It shows in their countenance.

Verses 10-11

Verse 12

This verse refers to the organization and partnership of the family.

Some scholars have also suggested that "women" in this context could be used to describe cowardly men.

Verses 13-15

The Lord is chastising the people for a lack of compassion and charity given to those in need and, in fact, make life more difficult for those who are suffering.

Verses 16-17

Scholars agree that "daughter of Zion" refers to one who lived in Jerusalem during Isaiah's day. Daughters of Zion (plural) could refer to his day as well as the last days.

Isaiah is describing the covenant daughters of Zion, who rather than keeping themselves pure and modest, are adorning themselves to look as the women of the world or their neighboring countries.

Many of the fashions of Isaiah's day are different than today; however, women (and men) choosing fashions to appear a certain way is a timeless issue.

In these (and the following verses) Isaiah specifically mentions ladies' jewelry and fashions that were popular in his day. Although it may be intriguing to discuss what each thing may have been, or what it could have looked like, the important principle is that the things she places so much value, time, and energy on has no eternal significance and will not sustain her.

"Smite with a scab the crown of the head" means to cause a disease of the scalp which would result in baldness. Hence, their appearance, which they value so much, will be taken away, or will not offer her happiness.

Verses 18-23

In Isaiah's day, the poor wore clothing made from their own sheep and often went without shoes. Isaiah is exposing the upper class of women who flaunt their jewelry and ornaments and take on the fashions of neighboring countries.

Verse 24

The details of this verse paints a picture of someone who is in mourning. In Isaiah's day, if someone was in mourning they would rent (rip) their clothing, shave their head, put on clothing made of sack cloth (an itchy material), and sit on the ground and sprinkle ashes over their head. They were outwardly doing things that expressed how they felt inwardly.

Verses 25-26

"Sit upon the ground" suggests that these women will be in great mourning. Where do we go when in distress? Often to the ground or lowest point.

2 NEPHI 14

Tip

In this chapter, Nephi continues to quote Isaiah. Isaiah is teaching about Zion and the Millennium.

In these boxes, doodle what you learn in each set of verses. Write what is happening, draw pictures, make diagrams, write definitions, ask questions, record your insights, or record quotes from latter-day prophets that teach about similar issues in our day.

Verse 1

Many scholars suggest that this verse could have been placed at the end of the previous chapter.

In Isaiah's day, it was disgraceful to be unmarried and childless. Due to the loss of men (through war or other means) the women ask the men to marry them without needing to fulfill the man's responsibility of providing for their needs.

Verse 2

Chapter 13 teaches about the widespread wickedness, pride, and despair. Chapter 14 prophesies of the redemption and cleansing of Israel and the establishment of Zion, even in the midst of a wicked world. There is a stark contrast between the despair of the world and hope in Christ and Zion.

The branch can either represent Christ or the House of Israel.

Verse 3

There are those who have abandoned the ways of the world and have had it's filth washed away.

Verse 4

Verse 5

"Upon every dwelling place": this can represent every church, temple, and home.
"Cloud and smoke": this is a protection for those in Zion from the heat or consequences of the world. This cloud would also shield the world from the glory of the Lord that is within the dwelling places.

Verse 6

Zion will be a place of refuge or the only place of peace and protection during a time that the world is in great turmoil.

2 NEPHI 15 _____

Tip

In this chapter, Nephi continues to quote Isaiah. At the beginning of this chapter Isaiah is comparing the House of Israel to a vineyard.

In these boxes, doodle what you learn in each set of verses. Write what is happening, draw pictures, make diagrams, write definitions, ask questions, record your insights, or record quotes from latter-day prophets that teach about similar issues in our day.

Verse 1

- This chapter uses the vineyard and the grapevines in the vineyard to represent the House of Israel.
- The grapevine is capable of producing a lot of fruit if given the required care and attention. If left uncared for, it will seldom survive.
- These characteristics made the grapevine a good comparison to the House of Israel.
- the "well-beloved" is Christ who is caring for this vineyard (the House of Israel).

Verse 2

It was a very fruitful hill where the vineyard was planted. The result should have been an abundant harvest but, instead, wild grapes grew.

Verses 3-4

Verse 5

Since this vineyard failed to produce, this is what will happen to it.

Verse 6

Verse 7

Tip

Verses 8-23 proclaim six woeful behaviors and consequences among the House of Israel.

Verses 8-9

Wo #1

Wealthy land owners would buy up all of the property they could until their borders met up with one another's. This violated the Law of Jubilee which protected people from being enslaved to the wealthy who had no intention of using the land for good.

Bible Dictionary: "Jubilee, Year of"

Verse 10

The consequence is that these lands would become extremely unproductive.

1 Homer = 10 Ephah
Therefore, the land owner would get 1/10th back of what he planted; and therefore would have a great loss.

1 Bath = 4-8 gallons of wine
4-8 gallons of wine over 10 acres of land is a ridiculously small harvest.

Verses 11-12

Wo #2

Isaiah is describing people who were the "partiers" of his day. The musical instruments were used in worship, but these people were using them at their feasts.

Verses 13-14

The result is a spiritual and intellectual famine among the people.

Hell, who has deceived them all along, will happily receive them.

Verses 15-16

Verse 17

Isaiah has taught about the waste of land and the waste of intellect. These places and people are left desolate. Imagine a desolate field which has stopped producing fruit or crop. What is left? Forage for lambs and young goats ("strangers" can be translated as young goats).

Verses 18-19	Wo #3
A cart rope is a rope that is pulling a cart filled with something. Here, the rope is pulling sin and vanity. "That we may see it" means that they are sign seekers. They are telling the Lord to hurry and show them so that they can know it.	

Verse 20	Wo #4
The great switch of values and change of perception of good and evil.	

Verse 21	Wo #5

Verses 22-23	Wo #6
Who justify the wicked for reward" are those who take bribes. Verse 22 teaches about alcohol or harmful products. Some scholars suggest that Isaiah is referring to those in our day who will promote dangerous or immoral products in exchange for large amounts of money. This type of advertising, especially when targeting youth, leads individuals away from righteousness.	

Verses 24-26	
- When a farmer has gathered his grain he would wait for a windy day and "winnow" his grain. He did this to separate the seeds from the "chaff" and "stubble". He would gather it and toss it in the air. The wind would then blow the lighter chaff and stubble away while the seed would fall back to the ground. Once the farmer gathered his seed he would burn the chaff and stubble with a fire that would grow extremely fast. Isaiah is likening the fate of the chaff and stubble to those who fall within the 6 woes. - An ensign is flag or "standard" raised during times of battle. - The Hebrew translation for "hiss" is to quietly proclaim.	

Verses 27-30	
Isaiah is describing the speed and haste in which the people will gather. Many scholars suggest that Isaiah is trying to describe the transportation of the last days and how the people can arrive in little time, without stopping to sleep. The quality of a horse depended, partly, on how hard their hooves were. Flint is a hard type of quartz. Many sholars suggest that Isaiah was seeing an unstoppable, powerful means of transportation. The wheels of a whirlwind could be a train and the roaring of a lion could be a plane's powerful engine.	

2 NEPHI 16

Tip

In this chapter, Nephi continues to quote Isaiah. Isaiah is writing about his calling to become the prophet.

Verse 1

-Isaiah is having a vision and will attempt to describe what he is seeing using figurative language. This is often how prophets seek to explain the grandeur and splendor of such a moment.

- Consider each thing literally and figuratively. For example, was the Lord actually sitting upon a throne? Maybe, maybe not. If not, what would the throne represent?

- A train is something that follows behind, like a train on a wedding gown. The longer the train, the greater the symbol of glory. The train could also represent the Lord's followers.

Verse 2

Wings are symbols of power and these beings had three sets of these wings. One set covered their faces, another set covered their feet, and with the last set they could fly.

Verses 3-4

These seraphim cried with such power that the posts of the door shook. The doorway should be the most solid part of the building, and even this is moved by the power of these voices.

The smoke could represent the prayers sent up from earth. In the ancient tabernacles, the Priests would stand before the Altar of Incense and pray in behalf of the Children of Israel. That smoke arising up from the altar was representative of their prayers going up to heaven. Here, Isaiah sees that the prayers have made it before the Lord.

Verses 5-7

Isaiah looks around and realizes that he feels out of place there. He is un-done, or not ready.

The live, or hot, coal from the altar would have come from the Altar of Sacrifice which was representative of the Savior's Atonement. This coal would have burned or cleansed Isaiah's sin away.

Verses 8-10

The last part of verse 10 could be misunderstood to say that the Lord does not want the people to be converted. Rather, this verse is saying that the people did not want to see, hear, or understand because they might be converted if they did. The first part of the verse counsels Isaiah to make the truth so clear that they cannot avoid it. The last part is referring to their attitude.

Verses 11-13

A teil-tree and an oak tree are both trees that cannot just be cut down. New life will shoot forth from their trunks and the tree will regenerate. So, though Israel will be "eaten" they will come forth again.

"Eaten" is a term that represents the enemy coming and consuming them.

2 NEPHI 17

Title for this chapter

In this chapter, Nephi continues to quote Isaiah. Isaiah is writing about counseling the King of Judah, King Ahaz.

Verses 1-2

- Ahaz is the King of Judah
- Pekah is the King of Israel (Ephraim)
- Rezin is the King of Syria
- Judah and Israel have divided from each other and set their own kings in place. Israel lives in the northern part of Israel, and Judah in the south.
- The King of Israel and the King of Syria were forming an alliance and combining forces against Assryia. Assryia was battling nations as they tried to enlarge their borders. The kings of Israel and Syria wanted King Ahaz to join with them.

Verses 3-4

- The Lord tells Isaiah to prophesy to Ahaz and counsel him not to join Israel and Syria, but rather to trust that the Lord will protect Judah from Assyria.
- Isaiah met King Ahaz at the springs because the king would be supervising means to protect their water supply.
- Firebrands were torches. In this case it is the tail of the kings, and their torches have gone out and are now smoking. This represented that their power was now gone.

Verses 5-6

Isaiah knows the plans of Syria and Israel. Their plan was to replace King Ahaz with a king of their choosing who would form the alliance with them.

Verses 7-9

Isaiah is prophesying of Ephraim's (Israel's) future. Judah and Israel had divided and Israel had gone north and established their own king. Isaiah knows that Israel will be taken captive, which history shows does happen. Assyria will come and deport most of the people to other countries. This is the beginning of the scattering of Israel.

Verses 10-13

Verses 14-15

The Lord gives Ahaz a sign and explains that his land has a great destiny to fulfill.

Butter and honey were foods that children particularly liked.

Verses 16-17

These verses (14-16) are what is known as a dual prophecy, which Isaiah did often. He was teaching of the Savior who would be born, but also of a child born in his day (most likely his own son). This child would not be very old before Assyria would overtake their land.

Verses 18-19

Bees and flies symbolized soldiers coming to battle. This is referring to the ruthless Assyrian army.

Verse 20

War prisoners were often forced into slavery and shaven from head to toe, which was humiliating to them and their Jewish customs.

Verses 21-23

Those left behind shall only have a few animals and so their main diet will be milk, honey and butter.

Verses 24-25

Only hunters will venture into the thorns seeking meat for food.

A mattock is a hoe. These hills, which were once so cared for and cultivated, will be only left for their few grazing cattle, rather than for crops.

Tip

In this chapter, Nephi continues to quote Isaiah. After King Ahaz's refusal to listen to Isaiah, Isaiah then turns to counsel the people.

Verses 1-4	
Since Ahaz refused to heed Isaiah's counsel, Isaiah will now turn to the people and try to get them to obey the Lord. Isaiah has two sons: Maher-sha-lal-hash-baz and Shear-jashub. Isaiah's wife, the prophetess, gives birth to Maher-sha-lal-hash-baz. This name means "to speed the spoil" which was the fate of Judah.	

Verses 5-8	
The waters of Shiloah were gentle, flowing waters that provided life-sustaining water to the inhabitants of Jerusalem. In this context, the waters symbolized the Lord's guidance and the spiritual source for the people. Since the people are rejecting this source, another river (the Assyrians) will flood their land and gather around their necks.	

Verses 9-12	
Whenever a phrase is repeated, the message is given extra emphasis. Isaiah is warning the people against joining with Israel and Syria and combining forces against Assyria.	

Verses 13-15	
The Lord can be a protective rock of offense, or a sanctuary. But the people of Isaiah's day saw Him as a stumbling block, or as someone who was getting in their way.	

Verses 16-18	
These prophecies, now recorded, are a witness against the people.	

Verses 19-22	
These verses warn of seeking after other sources of spiritual guidance. If they do so, they will be led astray. Isaiah has recorded these words (the law and testimony), and any other forms of spiritualism will bring trouble and darkness.	

2 NEPHI 19

Tip

In this chapter, Nephi continues to quote Isaiah. Isaiah prophesies of the future Messiah and of evils that will bring destruction.

Verse 1

- Chapters 19 and 20 are natural continuations fo chapters 17 and 18. The context centers on the threat of an Assyrian invasion.
- In 17 and 18 Isaiah warns Ahaz and the people of what would happen if they formed an alliance with Israel and Syria.
- Chapters 19 and 20 are more detailed prophecies. Since Ahaz ignored Isaiah's warnings. the alliance has now happened.
- The Land of Israel was divided as an inheritance for the descendants of the 12 tribes of Israel. Zebulun and Naphtali were given land in the northern part of Israel which bordered other nations. Their lands were known as the "Galilee of Nations" because there was a lot of mixed nationality. These lands were the first to be captured by Assyria.

Verses 2-5

These lands will see hard days but will yet experience greatness.

The Assyrians will come and take the lands, but the Lord will ultimately devastate their armies and the land of Israel will still fulfill its destiny.

Verses 6-7

This is a dual prophecy. These verses speak of Christ as well as King Hezekiah. King Hezekiah was a righteous king who listened to Isaiah and tried to turn the people to the Lord.

Verses 8-12 | PRIDE

- Verses 8-20 mention evils that will be destroyed and ultimately bring destruction to the people.
- These are dual prophecies. They are speaking of the destruction in Isaiah's day as well as those preceding the Second Coming.
- The people thought that they were strong enough and could replace everything that was destroyed with better things. Bricks were man-made and were inferior to hewn (carved out) stones. Cedar wood was superior to sycamore wood.

Verses 13-17 | WICKED LEADERS

These verses are referencing the wicked leadership. The head is government leaders and the tail is false prophets.

Verses 18-21 | WICKEDNESS

Wickedness is compared to a forest fire that spreads everywhere using the people as fuel.

2 NEPHI 20

In this chapter, Nephi continues to quote Isaiah. Isaiah writes about the destruction of Assyria.

In these boxes, doodle what you learn in each set of verses. Write what is happening, draw pictures, make diagrams, write definitions, ask questions, record your insights, or record quotes from latter-day prophets that teach about similar issues in our day.

Verses 1-4

TURNING AWAY THOSE IN NEED

The fourth evil from the previous chapter is in the first four verses in this chapter.

Isaiah is talking about people that turn away those in need. In verse 3 he directed questions to these people. They who turned away so many, who will THEY turn to and ask for help when the destruction comes?

Verses 5-6

These verses prophesy of the destruction of Assyria, a nation who thought themselves to be all powerful.

The Lord calls Assyria the "rod of my anger". The Lord used Assyria to humble his people, the rod being a symbol of something that smites or strikes. If Israel and Judah would have turned to the Lord, He would have protected them from Assyria.

Verse 7

Assyria's intention was not to assist God but to cut down many nations for their own gain. They did not intend to further God's purposes.

Verses 8-11

"Are not my princes altogether kings?" - Assyria is boasting that even their army commanders are as powerful as kings.

The King of Assyria is, again, boasting in this verse as he looked over his conquered cities. He is saying, "Should I not also do this to Jerusalem?"

Verses 12-14

The Lord will punish Assyria who thinks that it has accomplished everything through its own power.

In verse 14, Israel is compared to a bird in its nest. The eggs in the nest represent the riches of Israel. The bird is Israel who cannot make a sound or move its wings. It is in a helpless condition with the Assyrian armies.

Verse 15

The ax is Assyria and the person holding the ax is the Lord. But the ax is the one taking all of the credit.

Verses 16-19

Assyria will be destroyed like a forest fire that destroys a forest in a single day. The thorns and briers are metaphors for wickedness and sin that provide fuel for this fire. The fire will be so complete that a child can count the trees that remain standing.

Verses 20-22

These verses prophesy of the gathering of Israel in the last days.

Israel is gathered by being baptized into the Gospel. The House of Israel are those that are heirs of the Abrahamic Covenant and all of the promises held in that covenant. They also hold the responsibility to take the Gospel to the world.

Verse 23

The Lord shall "make a consumption" which means that there will be a judgment / consumption that will happen to the world. The gathered remnant of Israel have a little bit of time to gather as many of the House of Israel as possible (on both sides of the veil).

Verses 24-26

"My people that dwellest in Zion" is a plea for the Lord's people to trust Him, although they may be temporarily under the rule of a nation such as the Assyrians.

Verses 27-32

Isaiah is giving a graphic description of the Assyrians' advancing armies (which is representative of wicked nations in the last days). They are getting closer and closer to Jerusalem as they pass through city after city. Isaiah does this in a way to help us feel the fear and anxiety as the situation seems more and more fearful.

Verses 33-34

There is sudden destruction of Assyria (or the wicked in the last days) and the righteous are spared.

2 NEPHI 21-22

Title for this chapter

Tip

Nephi continues to quote Isaiah. Isaiah is teaching about the last days and the Millennium.

21:1

The "stem of Jesse" is the Mortal Messiah. Jesse was King David's father and the Messiah was prophesied to come through that kingly line which was known as the Davidic Line. Mary was a descendant of David.

Some scholars suggest that the "rod" and the "branch" is Joseph Smith.

This verse is a continuation of the previous chapter. The Lord will cut down the forest and replace it with a righteous tree.

21:2-5

These verses teach about Christ during the Millennium.

21:6-9

Little children will have wisdom and understanding that others can learn from.

"The earth shall be full of knowledge": some scholars suggest that this teaches the desire for people to have knowledge along with the technological advancements providing that knowledge.

21:10-12

This verse teaches about the gathering of Israel and the Church of Jesus Christ of Latter-Day Saints standing as an Ensign to gather them.

21:13-14

Judah (the Southern Kingdom of Israel) and Ephraim (the Northern Kingdom of Israel) who were once divided, will now be at peace with one another.

"Fly upon the shoulders of the Philistines": the Philistines in this verse mean the Gentiles. These Gentiles will invent great means for travel and communication.

Verse 14 mention Israel's former enemies. In the last days, they represent any nation who stands in the way of God and His ways.

21:15-16

"Tongue" in verse 15 can also mean "gulf".

These verses reference Moses leading the Israelites out of Egypt and across the Red Sea. This is symbolic of nations being unable to interfere with the Lord's work and the gathering of His people.

22:1-6

These verses contain two short psalms. The first psalm is found in verses 1-3, and the second in verses 4-6.

59

Tip

Nephi continues to quote Isaiah. Isaiah prophecies about the destruction of Babylon and the destruction at the Second Coming.

verses 1-2

-Babylon was a symbol of the wickedness of the world. This chapter contains a dual prophecy (the destruction of Babylon which is like the destruction of the world at the Second Coming of Jesus Christ).
- Some scholars suggest the banner (which is an Ensign) is the Book of Mormon.
- "Go into the gates": This is an invitation to enter into the Holy City (Jerusalem or New Jerusalem).

verses 3-5

-Sanctified Ones: those that are temple worthy
- "Noise" can also be translated as "voice"
- Speaking of these verses, Joseph Smith said. "This has reference to gathering of the Saints in the Rocky Mountains." (Teachings of the Prophet Joseph Smith, 255).

verses 6-9

-"Their faces shall be as flames": This can mean that they are experiencing intense pain or are red with shame.

verses 10-12

"I will make a man more precious than fine gold": so great will be the destruction that those who survive will be as fine gold.

- Ophir was a fine gold that kings would import.

verses 13-16

- A "roe" is likely a gazelle

verses 17-19

"The Medes" were an army from Persia that had successffully crushed Babylon.

"Chaldees" is a name often used to describe Babylonians.

verses 20-22

The fate of Babylon or the wickedness of the world.

2 NEPHI 24

Tip	
Nephi continues to quote Isaiah. Isaiah prophecies about what it will be like during the Millennium.	

verses 1-3	
-"Strangers shall be joined with them" refers to the uniting of the House of Israel and Gentiles in holiness.	

verses 4-8	
- Verse 4 begins as a poem or song meant to be sung to the King of Babylon (who represents the head of wickedness of the world). - Even the Cedars of Lebanon feel at peace since destruction has ceased.	

verses 9-11	
- Satan will be bound during the Millennium. This part of the poem talks about the reaction of men and women in hell when they realize Satan is there, just as they are.	

verses 12-17	

verses 18-20	

verses 21-23	
- The destruction of Babylon / the world	

verses 24-27	

verses 28-32	
-Palestina was a flourishing and wealthy city that enjoyed much prosperity. - The serpent's root, the cockatrice, and the fiery flying serpent are all symbols of evil that will ultimately come upon them.	

2 NEPHI 25 _____

Title for this chapter

Tip

Nephi is no longer quoting Isaiah and is now commenting on Isaiah's writings.

5 POINTS

In this box doodle five points you find in verses 1-3

ISAIAH'S WORDS

Study verses 4-8 and then in this box doodle what you learn about the words of Isaiah and how to understand them.

"AND NEVER HATH..."

In this box doodle the last phrase of verse 9 starting with "and never". Write what this phrase means to you in this context.

FUTURE EVENTS IN JERUSALEM

In this box record the future events in Jerusalem foretold in verses 10-17.

Study the following verses and search for an important doctrine or teaching in each verse. Record what you learn from these verses.

18	19
20	21
22	23
Before studying the next verse(s), look up "Law of Moses" in the Bible Dictionary and explain what you learned here.	24
25	26
27	28
29	30

2 NEPHI 26

Title for this chapter

Nephi is prophesying to the Nephites. What are some specific things he tells them in verses 1-3. Doodle what you find here.

What will happen to the wicked and to the righteous when the resurrected Christ comes to the Nephites?

THE WICKED	THE RIGHTEOUS
Verses 3-7	Verses 8-9

In this box, doodle specific things you learn in verses 10-15.

Doodle what you learn in the prophecy about the Book of Mormon in verses 16-17.

Study verses 18-33. Doodle what you learn in those verses. Try to include at least one thing from each verse.

2 NEPHI 27

THE LAST DAYS

Doodle what you learn about the LAST DAYS in verses 1-5.

Tip

THE BOOK OF MORMON

What is the sealed portion?

According to those who saw the plates, anywhere from half to two-thirds of the plates were sealed. Moroni was commanded to seal up parts of the plates and Joseph was commanded not to translate the sealed portion. We know that the sealed portion contains the following:

- The full record of the vision the Brother of Jared had including the history of mankind (Ether 3:25-27; 4:4-5)
- "All things from the foundation of the world to the end thereof" (2 Nephi 27:10-11)

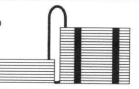

 What do you learn about the Book of Mormon in verses 6-11 and 21-22?

OLIVER COWDERY DAVID WHITMER MARTIN HARRIS

What do you learn about the three witnesses of the Book of Mormon in verses 12-14?

Doodle about the prophesy in verses 15-20.

Read about the fulfillment of this prophecy in Joseph-Smith History 1:63-65. Doodle the details of what happened.

Study verses 23-35 and doodle the doctrines and principles you find in each verse.

23	24	25	26
27	28	29	30
31-32	33	34	35

2 NEPHI 28

Title for this chapter

THE LAST DAYS

Doodle what you learn in these verses about the last days.

The Book of Mormon	False Churches	False Teachings	False Teachings
1-2	3-4	5-6	7-9

Corrupt Men & Churches	Corrupt Men & Churches	Woe's	Kingdom of the Devil
10-12	13-14	15-17	18-19

Satan's Tactics
Verses 20-22 reveal some of the tactics that Satan will use to get individuals to follow him. Doodle what you find in these verses.

Verse 20	Verse 21	Verse 22

Satan's Goal
What do verses 22-23 teach you about Satan's goals?

Doodle what you learn in these verses about the last days.

Doodle what you learn in these verses about the last days.

Wo #1	Wo #2	Wo #3	Wo #4
24	25	26	27

Wo #5	Wo #6	How God reveals his word	Wo #7
28	29	30	31-32

2 NEPHI 29 _____

THE LAST DAYS

A
Marvelous
WORK

Read verses 1-2 and in this box. doodle about why the Lord will do a "marvelous work" in the last days.

Study verse 3 and record what Nephi prophesies what people will say when the Book of Mormon comes forth.

_____
_____
_____
_____

Study verses 4-14 which is the Lord's response to what the people said in verse 3. Doodle some of the main points you find in the spaces below.

Verse 4	Verse 5	Verses 6-7
Verse 8	**Verse 9**	**Verses 10-11**
Verse 12	**Verse 13**	**Verse 14**

2 NEPHI 30 _____
Title for this chapter

THE LAST DAYS

What prophecies, doctrines, and principles do you learn in these verses? Doodle what you find in each box.

Verses 1-2	Verses 3-4	Verses 5-6
		* Restoration *

Verses 7-8	Verses 9-10	Verses 11-12

Verses 13-14	Verses 15-16	Verses 17-18

2 NEPHI 31 _____

What do you learn from Nephi in verses 1-3?

Title for this chapter

VERSE 1	VERSE 2	VERSE 3

The
Baptism
of
Jesus Christ

Doodle what you learn about the baptism of Christ in verses 4-9.

_____

Study verses 10-21 and fill this space as you doodle the DOCTRINES OF CHRIST that you learn. Try to include at least one thing from each verse.

Doctrines of Christ

Doctrines of Christ

Study this chapter and fill this page as you doodle the DOCTRINES OF CHRIST that you learn. Try to include at least one thing from each verse.

2 NEPHI 33

The Holy Ghost

Study verses 1 and 2. In this box, doodle what you learn about the Holy Ghost.

Nephi's testimony of his writings

Study verses 3-5. Doodle some of your favorite phrases from these verses. Include what those phrases teach you about Nephi and/or his writings.

Qualities of Nephi

Doodle the qualities of Nephi you can find in verses 6-9.

Favorite Phrases

Study verses 10-15. Pick 5 phrases that stand out to you. Doodle them here and include what you like about them.

JACOB 1 _____

Title for this chapter

Read verse 1 and then in this box, record how many years it had been since Lehi had led his family out of Jerusalem.

Look at the lower right corner of the page in Jacob 1. Record the date in the parentheses in this box.

1-4 Doodle Nephi's command he gave to his brother Jacob.

5-6 Doodle what you learn about Joseph and Jacob in these verses.

7 Doodle what Joseph and Jacob did in this verse.

8 Doodle about what Joseph and Jacob desired.

9-14 Doodle what happens in these verses.

15-16 Doodle what happens in these verses.

17-19 Doodle about what Jacob and Joseph did.

Lessons Learned from Nephi

Doodle some lessons you have learned from Nephi throughout 1 and 2 Nephi.

71

JACOB 2

Title for this chapter

Study Jacob 2 and fill the boxes below with doodles of the doctrines and principles you find.

VERSES 1-5	VERSES 6-7

VERSES 8-9	VERSES 10-11

VERSES 12-13	VERSES 14-16

VERSE 17	VERSES 18-19

VERSES 20-21	VERSES 22-23

VERSES 24-28	VERSES 29-30

VERSES 31-33	VERSES 34-35

JACOB 3

Doodle what you learn from Jacob's teachings in the boxes below.

The Pure in Heart
Verses 1-2

The Not Pure in Heart
Verses 3-4, 8-12

The Lamanites
Verses 5-7

Jacob's Record
Verses 13-14

73

JACOB 4 _____

Doodle what you learn from Jacob's teachings in the boxes below.

What Jacob can write	Jacob's hope
1-2	3-4

The words of prophets that came before Jacob	Despise not the revelations from God
5-6	7-8

The power of the word	Be reconciled through the Atonement
9-10	11

Why not speak of the Atonement?	TRUTH
12	13

Looking beyond the mark	The sure foundation
14-15	16-18

JACOB 5

Tip

Jacob had studied the words of the prophets on the brass plates. On those plates there were the writings of the prophet Zenos whose record we no longer have. While Jacob was teaching the people, he quoted "The Allegory of the Tame and Wild Olive Trees" which Zenos had originally recorded.

As you study Jacob 5, follow along the boxes below. As you study doodle notes, details, pictures, questions, etc.

First Visit — Verses 1-14

Verses 1-3	Verses 4-6	Verse 7
Tame olive tree is dying	Efforts put forth to save the tree. New branches come but top is still dying.	Dying branches are burned.

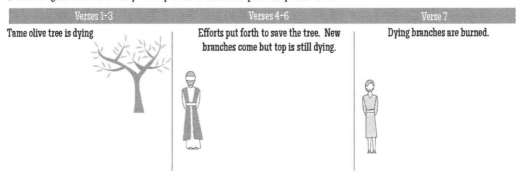

Verse 8, 13-14	What is Grafting?	Verse 7, 9-12
Many new branches grafted into other trees.	"Grafting" was a common practice in ancient times where you would take a branch from one tree and insert it into a different tree. One purpose of doing this might be to help an olive tree which was no longer bearing fruit. One would take a branch from a healthy tree and "Graft" it into the wild tree in hopes that it would strengthen the tree.	Wild branches grafted into tame tree.

Second Visit — Verses 15-28

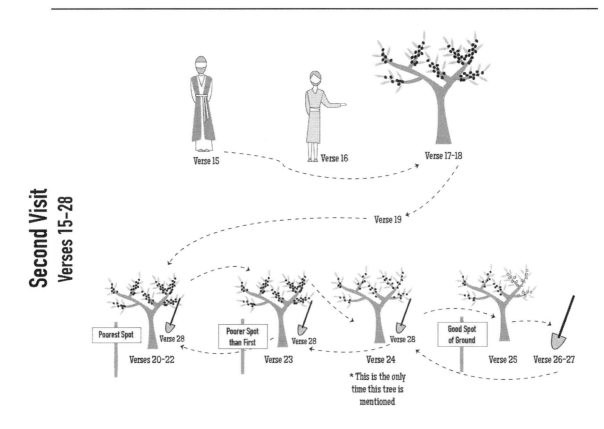

Verse 15

Verse 16

Verse 17-18

Verse 19

Poorest Spot — Verse 28 — Verses 20-22

Poorer Spot than First — Verse 28 — Verse 23

Verse 28 — Verse 24

Good Spot of Ground — Verse 25 — Verse 26-27

* This is the only time this tree is mentioned

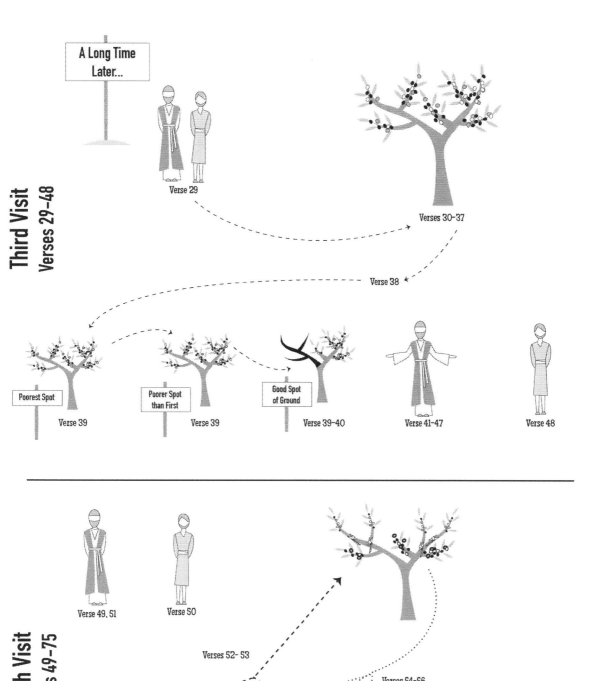

Third Visit
Verses 29-48

A Long Time Later...

Verse 29

Verses 30-37

Verse 38

Poorest Spot

Verse 39

Poorer Spot than First

Verse 39

Good Spot of Ground

Verse 39-40

Verse 41-47

Verse 48

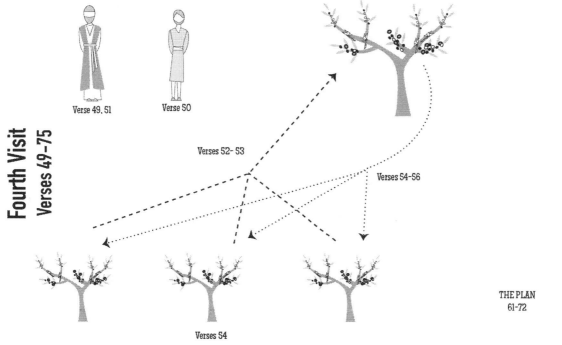

Fourth Visit
Verses 49-75

Verse 49, 51

Verse 50

Verses 52- 53

Verses 54-56

Verses 54

THE PLAN
61-72

Instructions	Goals	The Plan	The Results
57-58	59-60	61-72	73-77

What does the first visit teach you about the SCATTERING OF ISRAEL?

How could the branches grafted into the tame olive tree represent the GENTILES?

What does the last visit teach you about the GATHERING OF ISRAEL?

How could the tree that was planted on the "good spot of ground" be the Nephites and Lamanites?

How could the third visit represent Christianity during the GREAT APOSTASY?

What are some phrases in Jacob 5 that show us how much the Lord cares about us?

JACOB 6

Study verses 1-4. In this box doodle what you learn about the Lord recovering Israel in the last days.

Study verses 5-8. Jacob is pleading for the Nephites to repent. Doodle some of your favorite phrases and questions he uses as he tries to touch their hearts.

Study verses 9-13. What warnings does Jacob give those who refuse to repent? Doodle what you find here.

If you had to choose one phrase from this chapter to give a talk on at church, which one might you choose? Why did you choose it?

JACOB 7

In this chapter Jacob encounters a man named Sherem who denies Christ. Doodle what is happening, said, or taught in each box below.

Sherem	Sherem	Sherem seeks to shake Jacob's faith
1-2	3-4	5

Sherem's deceitful words	Sherem's deceitful words	Question / Answer
6-7	8	9

Question / Answer	Jacob testifies	Sherem asks for a sign
10	11-12	13-15

Sherem admits to people he was wrong	Sherem dies	Peace and love restored
16-19	20-21	22-23

The Lamanites	Jacob's last words	Jacob gives plates to son Enos
24-25	26	27

ENOS _____
Title for this chapter

As you study the Book of Enos, doodle what you learn in the appropriate boxes.

Enos' concerns, questions, and desires

Doctrines, Principles and Lessons I learn in this chapter

What I learn about the Nephites and Lamanites

JAROM

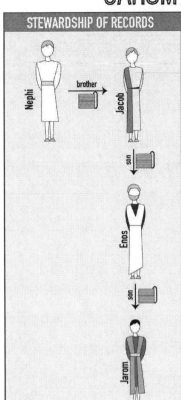

STEWARDSHIP OF RECORDS

As you study the Book of Jarom, doodle 15 important facts, teachings or principles. Try to include one from each verse.

1

2

3

4

5

6

7

8

9

10

11

12

13

14

15

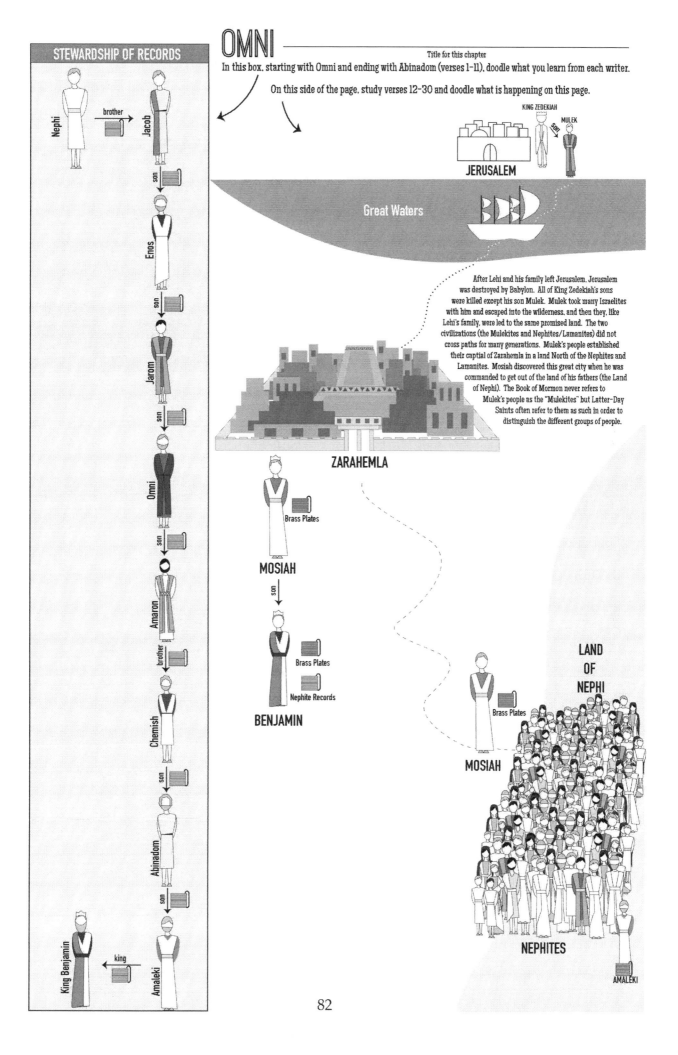

STEWARDSHIP OF RECORDS

Nephi

brother

Jacob

son

Enos

son

Jarom

son

Omni

son

Amaron

brother

Chemish

son

Abinadom

son

Amaleki

king

King Benjamin

OMNI

Title for this chapter

In this box, starting with Omni and ending with Abinadom (verses 1-11), doodle what you learn from each writer.

On this side of the page, study verses 12-30 and doodle what is happening on this page.

KING ZEDEKIAH

MULEK
son

JERUSALEM

Great Waters

After Lehi and his family left Jerusalem, Jerusalem was destroyed by Babylon. All of King Zedekiah's sons were killed except his son Mulek. Mulek took many Israelites with him and escaped into the wilderness, and then they, like Lehi's family, were led to the same promised land. The two civilizations (the Mulekites and Nephites/Lamanites) did not cross paths for many generations. Mulek's people established their captial of Zarahemla in a land North of the Nephites and Lamanites. Mosiah discovered this great city when he was commanded to get out of the land of his fathers (the Land of Nephi). The Book of Mormon never refers to Mulek's people as the "Mulekites" but Latter-Day Saints often refer to them as such in order to distinguish the different groups of people.

ZARAHEMLA

Brass Plates

MOSIAH

son

Brass Plates

Nephite Records

BENJAMIN

Brass Plates

MOSIAH

LAND OF NEPHI

NEPHITES

AMALEKI

82

WORDS OF MORMON _____

Title for this chapter

Tip

This book, "The Words of Mormon," is like a pause in the record of the Nephites. At this point, Mormon was not yet alive; in fact, he will not live for over 500 years after the record of Omni was originally written. Mormon was the one who inherited all of the records and is "abridging" all of them into one set of plates.

Mormon is addressing the future readers of the plates. He expresses his desires for them as well as an explanation of the compilation and abridgments of the records from his ancestors.

DATE ON BOTTOM OF PAGE 142 _____

DATE ON BOTTOM OF PAGE 143 _____ = 515 YEARS LATER

Study Words of Mormon and doodle things he wanted us to know.

Verses 1-2	Verse 3	Verses 4-5

Verse 6	Verse 7	Verse 8

Verse 9	Verse 10	Verse 11

Verses 12-14	Verse 15-16	Verses 17-18

MOSIAH 1 _____

In this space, doodle everything you learn in verses 1-8.

BENJAMIN

MOSIAH **HELORUM** **HELAMAN**

Doodle what is happening n verses 9-12.

What warning does King Benjamin give Mosiah about the people in verses 13-14?

What did King Benjamin give to Mosiah in verses 15-17?

What did King Benjamin ask the people to do in verse 18?

MOSIAH 2 _____

Tip

Before King Benjamin dies, he calls his people together to speak to them. Chapters 2-5 contain his sermon to the people.

Study verses 1-8 and doodle what you learn about King Benjamin's people and what happened when he called them together.

Doodle what doctrines and principles you learn from King Benjamin's sermon in these boxes.

Verse 9	Verses 10-12	Verses 13-15	Verses 16-17
Verses 18-19	Verses 20-21	Verse 22	Verses 23-24
Verses 25-26	Verses 27-28	Verse 29-31	Verses 32-33
Verses 34-35	Verses 36-37	Verse 38-40	Verse 41

MOSIAH 3 _____

Doodle what doctrines and principles you learn from King Benjamin's sermon in these boxes.

Verse 1	Verses 2-4	Verse 5	Verses 6-8
			MESSIANIC PROPHECY

Verses 9-11	Verses 12-13	Verses 14-15	Verse 16
MESSIANIC PROPHECY			

Verse 17	Verse 18	Verse 19	Verses 20-22

Verses 23-24	Verse 25	Verse 26	Verse 27

MOSIAH 4 _____

Doodle what doctrines and principles you learn from King Benjamin's sermon in these boxes.

Verses 1-2	Verse 3	Verses 4-7	Verse 8
IMPACT OF DOCTRINE	POWER OF THE SPIRIT		

Verses 9-10	Verse 11	Verses 12-13	Verses 14-16

Verses 17-19	Verses 20-23	Verses 24-25	Verse 26
ARE WE NOT ALL BEGGARS			

Verse 27	Verse 28	Verses 29-30	Doodle your favorite phrase from this chapter.

MOSIAH 5

Doodle what is happening in verse 1 along with important principles you see.

What do you learn about conversion / change in verse 2?

"We" to "I"

Study verses 3-5. Change the "we" phrases that the people said to "I" and apply those phrases to yourself, and doodle them. You can change some of the specifics to better apply to you; for example, you can change "king" to "prophet".

Taking Upon the Name of Christ / Becoming Children of Christ

Study verses 6-15. In this space, doodle everything you learn about taking upon the name of Christ.

King Benjamin's Sermon

Look over chapters 2-5 and choose phrases that could be a personal motto for the following life scenarios. Doodle the mottos you chose by each scenario.

A Motto for:

YOUR FAMILY

A Motto for:

BEING A PARENT

A Motto for:

YOUR CALLING

A Motto for:

YOUTH CONFERENCE

A Motto for:

YOUR LIFE

A Motto for:

WARD / BRANCH

A Motto for:

YOUR MISSION

A Motto for:

BEING A FRIEND

MOSIAH 6 _____

Title for this chapter

VERSES 1-2 Doodle about the impact the sermon had on the people.

VERSE 3 Doodle about the affairs of the kingdom.

VERSES 4-7 Doodle about Mosiah becoming the next king.

KING MOSIAH I

son

KING BENJAMIN

son

KING MOSIAH II

MOSIAH 7

Tip

The Book of Mosiah can be confusing because it jumps back and forth to different time periods. Years before this point in King Mosiah II's life (2 generations before him), there was a group of Nephites who had left Zarahemla with the hopes of regaining the land of their fathers (the Land of Nephi). A man named Zeniff led them. That group of Nephites had not been heard of since; and King Mosiah II was concerned with their whereabouts and well-being, so he sent a search party to find them. Mosiah 7-8 is the journey of this group finding those lost Nephites. Mosiah 9-24 is the story of the Lost Nephites and what had happened once they left Zarahemla.

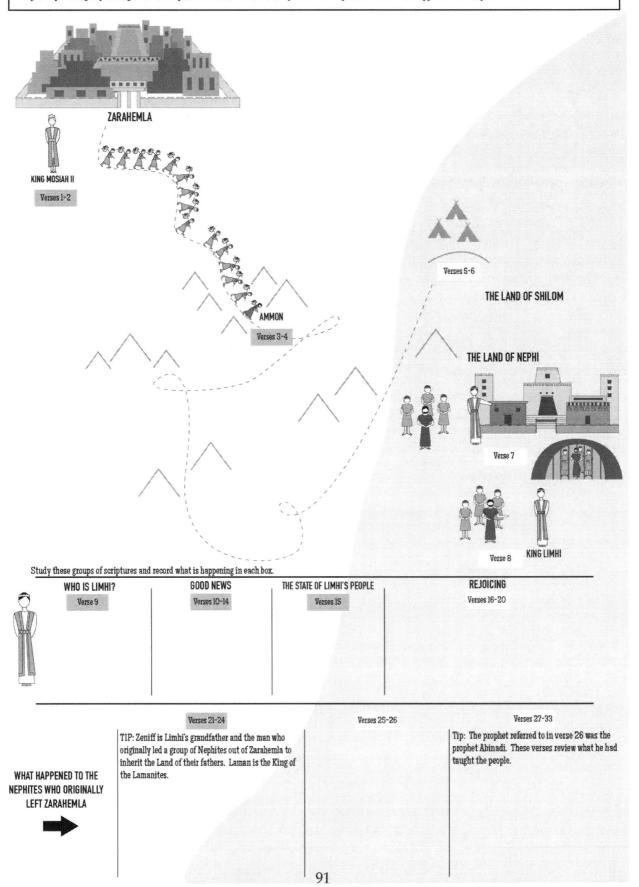

ZARAHEMLA

KING MOSIAH II

Verses 1-2

AMMON

Verses 3-4

Verses 5-6

THE LAND OF SHILOM

THE LAND OF NEPHI

Verse 7

Verse 8   KING LIMHI

Study these groups of scriptures and record what is happening in each box.

WHO IS LIMHI?	GOOD NEWS	THE STATE OF LIMHI'S PEOPLE	REJOICING
Verse 9	Verses 10-14	Verse 15	Verses 16-20

Verses 21-24

TIP: Zeniff is Limhi's grandfather and the man who originally led a group of Nephites out of Zarahemla to inherit the Land of their fathers. Laman is the King of the Lamanites.

Verses 25-26

Verses 27-33

Tip: The prophet referred to in verse 26 was the prophet Abinadi. These verses review what he had taught the people.

WHAT HAPPENED TO THE NEPHITES WHO ORIGINALLY LEFT ZARAHEMLA

➤

MOSIAH 8 _____

WHAT DID AMMON TEACH LIMHI'S PEOPLE?

Verses 1-4

WHAT DID LIMHI BRING BEFORE AMMON? WHY?

Verses 5-6

Study verses 7–11 and write on this story map what is happening.

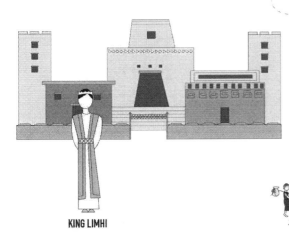

KING LIMHI

WHY DID LIMHI REJOICE?

Go back to chapter 7 and read verse 14 again. Now that you know about King Limhi sending 43 of his people off to find Zarahemla, why did he rejoice when he met Ammon and his brethren?

WHO COULD TRANSLATE THE 24 GOLD PLATES?

Verses 12-13 & Mosiah 28:17

WHAT IS A SEER?

Verses 14-19

WHAT DOCTRINES AND PRINCIPLES CAN YOU FIND IN VERSES 20–21?

Tip: "She" is referencing "wisdom" in the line before; so the line could read "...that wisdom should rule over them!".

MOSIAH 9

_____

Zeniff is the grandfather of Limhi and the one who originally left Zarahemla with a group of Nephites who wanted to take back the land of their fathers (the Land of Nephi). Remember in Omni we learned that King Mosiah I was inspired to lead the Nephites out of the Land of Nephi where they were under the constant threat of the Lamanites. Now these Nephites wanted to go back to that land where their fathers had lived. Mosiah 9 begins the record of what happened once they left, so you are jumping back in time starting in Mosiah 9 until Mosiah 21:22 as you learn about their history. This chapter begins at about 200 B.C. when Zeniff originally left Zarahemla. The chapter before when Ammon met Lehi was about 121 B.C., so Mosiah 9 is going back 79 years in time.

ANSWER THE FOLLOWING QUESTIONS ABOUT ZENIFF USING VERSES 1 AND 2.

1. What was Zeniff's job in the Nephite army?

2. What was Zeniff's dilemma in verse 1?

3. Why did a battle break out within Zeniff's own army?

4. Where did the survivors of the battle go?

_____

STUDY VERSES 3-9 AND WRITE AND DRAW WHAT IS HAPPENING ALL OVER THIS MAP.

ZENIFF

son

KING NOAH

son

KING LIMHI

THE LAND OF SHILOM

THE LAND OF NEPHI

KING LAMAN

ZENIFF

ZENIFF

STUDY THESE VERSES AND THEN IN EACH BOX, RECORD WHAT IS HAPPENING.

THE PLAN OF THE LAMANITE KING	12 YEARS LATER	THE LAMANITES
VERSE 10	VERSE 11	VERSES 12-13

LAMANITES ATTACK	ZENIFF'S RESPONSE	HOW TO GO TO BATTLE
VERSE 14	VERSE 15-17	VERSES 18-19

MOSIAH 10 _____

Title for this chapter

STUDY THESE VERSES AND RECORD WHAT IS HAPPENING IN EACH SPACE. YOU CAN ALSO
ADD PICTURES TO THE STORY MAPS.

ZENIFF'S LEADERSHIP
Verses 1-5

NEW LAMANITE KING
Verse 6

GUARDING THEMSELVES
Verse 7

LAMANITE ARMY
Verse 8

NEPHITE ARMY
Verse 9

HOW TO BATTLE
Verses 10-11

WHY THE LAMANITES HATED THE NEPHITES
Verses 12-18

HOW TO BATTLE
Verses 19-20

ZENIFF MAKES HIS SON KING
Verses 21-22

KING OF LAMANITES

THE LAND OF SHILOM

THE LAND OF NEPHI

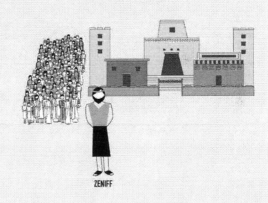

ZENIFF

MOSIAH 11 _____

Title for this chapter

WHAT DO YOU LEARN ABOUT KING NOAH AND THE NEPHITES HE REIGNED OVER? RECORD WHAT YOU FIND IN EACH BOX.

KING NOAH

VERSE 1	VERSE 2	VERSE 3	VERSE 4	VERSE 5
VERSE 6	VERSE 7	VERSE 8	VERSE 9	VERSE 10
VERSE 11	VERSE 12	VERSE 13	VERSE 14	VERSE 15

WHAT HAPPENED WHEN THE LAMANITES CAME UPON THE NEPHITES?	LESSONS LEARNED
Verses 16–18	What are some important teachings you see in verse 19?

WHAT IMPORTANT COUNSEL AND WARNINGS DID ABINADI GIVE THE PEOPLE?	WHAT WAS THE REACTION OF THE KING AND PEOPLE TO ABINADI?
Verses 20–25	Verses 26–29

MOSIAH 12

Title for this chapter

ABINADI

What do you learn about Abinadi's character and strength in verse 1?

List or draw specific prophesies Abinadi gave the people in verses 2-8.

How did the people react to Abinadi's prophesies? (verses 9-16) Record some of the foolish things they said.

Write or draw what happened in each of these verses:

 17

 18

 19

 20

Tip

The question that the council asks Abinadi is an interesting one. Are they really desiring an answer to this question or are they twisting Isaiah's words? Saying, "how beautiful upon the mountains are the feet of him that bringeth good tidings; that publish peace..." while Abinadi was prophesying such grave warnings. Were they really desiring Abinadi's opinion of that scripture, or were they trying to use scripture to condemn Abinadi?

THIS IS THE QUESTION THAT THE COUNCIL ASKED ABINADI. (VERSES 20-24)

What meaneth the words which are written, and which have been taught by our fathers saying:

How beautiful upon the mountains are the feet of him that bringeth good tidings; that publisheth peace; that bringeth good tidings of good; that publisheth salvation; that saith unto Zion, Thy God reigneth;

Thy watchmen shall lift up the voice; with the voice together shall they sing; for they shall see eye to eye when the Lord shall bring again Zion;

Break forth into joy; sing together ye waste places of Jerusalem; for the Lord hath comforted his people, he hath redeemed Jerusalem;

The Lord hath made bare his holy arm in the eyes of all the nations, and all the ends of the earth shall see the salvation of our God?

WHAT STANDS OUT TO YOU IN ABINADI'S ANSWER? VERSES 21-23

WHAT IS THEIR NEXT STATEMENT, AND HOW DID ABINADI REPLY TO THEM? VERSES 28-31

STUDY VERSES 32-37. ABINADI PUTS THE COUNCIL ON THE SPOT AND ASKS THEM HOW IMPORTANT THE COMMANDMENTS OF GOD ARE. NOTICE VERSE 37 AND COMPARE IT TO VERSE 32. WHAT POINT IS ABINADI MAKING TO THE COUNCIL?

WHAT IS FOOLISH ABOUT THE QUESTION AND STATEMENTS THE COUNCIL SAID TO ABINADI IN VERSES 20-24 AND 28?

MOSIAH 13 _____

ABINADI AND KING NOAH

MAKE AN OUTLINE OF THE CONVERSATION THAT HAPPENED IN VERSES 1-9. WE HAVE GIVEN YOU THE FIRST PART OF THE OUTLINE.

1- King Noah called Abinadi "mad" and said that they had to do away with him.

ABINADI'S TEACHINGS

NOTE THE IMPORTANT DOCTRINES AND PRINCIPLES THAT YOU FIND IN ABINADI'S WORDS IN THIS SERIOUS SITUATION.

VERSES 10-11

VERSES 12-14

VERSE 15

VERSES 16-19

VERSE 20

VERSE 21

VERSE 22

VERSE 23

VERSE 24

WHAT DOES ABINADI SAY IN VERSES 25 AND 26? WHAT DOES THIS TEACH YOU ABOUT ABINADI AND HIS STRENGTH AND COURAGE?

THE LAW OF MOSES

LOOK UP "LAW OF MOSES" IN YOUR BIBLE DICTIONARY AND TRY TO EXPLAIN WHAT IT IS IN A FEW SENTENCES.

STUDY VERSES 27-35, THEN LOOK AT THE QUESTIONS BELOW THAT SOMEONE MAY ASK YOU. ANSWER THEM USING THE DOCTRINES TAUGHT IN THOSE VERSES.

Is the Law of Moses the law that Saints will live forever?

Is living the Law of Moses what will bring us salvation and help us become like Christ?

Why did Moses give this law to the Children of Israel?

If we do not receive salvation through the Law of Moses, how will we receive it?

MOSIAH 14 _____

Tip

In the midst of Abinadi's teachings he quotes Isaiah. This particular prophecy of Isaiah is called a "Messianic Prophecy" which means it is a prophecy that teaches about the Messiah who will come and save all men. Abinadi quotes Isaiah in chapter 14 and then gives commentary on it in chapter 15.

Considering what Abinadi was teaching in the last chapter (Mosiah 13), why do you think he quoted a "Messianic Prophecy" from the prophet Isaiah, whom the council itself had just quoted in Mosiah 12:21-24?

In these boxes, doodle what you learn in each set of verses. Write what is happening, draw pictures, make diagrams, write definitions, ask questions, record your insights, or record quotes from latter-day prophets that teach about similar issues in our day.

14:1 - There are 2 questions in this verse that precede the verses that teach about a God coming to earth to be a mortal.	
14:2 - A tender plant is a young and vulnerable plant, like an innocent child. It is also not a grand plant that others may take notice of, like a king or person of great importance. - A plant does not usually take root in dry ground. The Jewish religion in his day was "dry". While there were many faithful Jews the leadership had become corrupt. - This verse does not necessarily suggest that Christ was unattractive, but that He did not stand out in a physical way.	
14:3-5 - Verse 3 prophecies of Christ's life and things He will face. - The word "borne" can also be translated as "forgiven".	
14:6 - When a sheep strays from his flock he has no sense of where he is and must be brought back by another source.	
14:7-8 -"Who shall declare his generation" refers to the Jewish tradition that one year after a father's death his son will "declare his generation," meaning that he will continue his father's seed. The son promises to carry on his father's legacy, family, and purpose.	
14:9-12 -"It pleased the Lord" can also be translated, "it was the will of the Lord".	

MOSIAH 15 _____

In these boxes, doodle what you learn from Abinadi in each set of verses. Write what is happening. draw pictures, make diagrams, write definitions, ask questions, record your insights, or record quotes from latter-day prophets that teach about similar issues in our day.

A God will become a mortal	The Father and the Son	Christ as the Father	
1-2	3-4	"... There are ways in which Christ is so united with his Father that in some assignments he rightfully plays a fatherly role and rightfully bears the title of Father in doing so. "This fundamental - and admittedly deep - doctrine of the Son-as-Father is illuminated more definitively in the Book of Mormon than in any other revelation ever given to man. "... First and foremost, as Abinadi taught, Christ was 'conceived by the power of God" and therefore has the powers of the Father within him. ...Christ also acts as the Father as he is the Creator of heaven and earth, is the father of our spiritual rebirth and salvation, and is faithful in honoring - and therefore claiming the power of- the will of his Father above that of his own will. Because of this inseparable relationship and uncompromised trust between them, Christ can at any time and in any place speak and act for the Father by virtue of the 'divine investiture of authority' the Father has given him." Elder Jeffrey R. Holland, *Christ and the New Covenant*, pp. 183-184	
Prophecy of Christ	**Prophecy of Christ**	**Explanation of "who shall declare his generation?"**	**Explanation of "who shall declare his generation?"**
5-7	8-9	10-13	14-18
Christ brings resurrection to all	**The First Resurrection**	**What is the First Resurrection?**	**Warning to those who die in sin**
19-20	21-25	"Those being resurrected with celestial bodies, whose destiny is to inherit a celestial kingdom, will come forth in the morning of the first resurrection. Their graves shall be opened and they shall be caught up to meet the Lord at his Second Coming. They are Christ's, the firstfruits, and they shall descend with him to reign as kings and priests during the millennial era." Elder Bruce R. McConkie *Mormon Doctrine*, p. 640	26-27
Prophecy	**Prophecy**	**Prophecy**	**Prophecy**
28	29	30	31

MOSIAH 16 _____

In these boxes, doodle what you learn from Abinadi in each set of verses. Write what is happening, draw pictures, make diagrams, write definitions, ask questions, record your insights, or record quotes from latter-day prophets that teach about similar issues in our day.

The time shall come...	Wicked will be cast out	Fallen Nature	The Fall
1	2	3	4

Those that persist in fallen nature	Need of Atonement	Christ's resurrection	Death swallowed up in Christ
5	6	7	8

A light that is endless	Judgment	Resurrection options	Resurrection of endless damnation
9	10	11	12

Ought ye not?	If ye teach the law of Moses...	Teach them...	Favorite phrases from this chapter
13	14	15	

MOSIAH 17 _____

Study verses 1–6 and write on this story map what is happening.

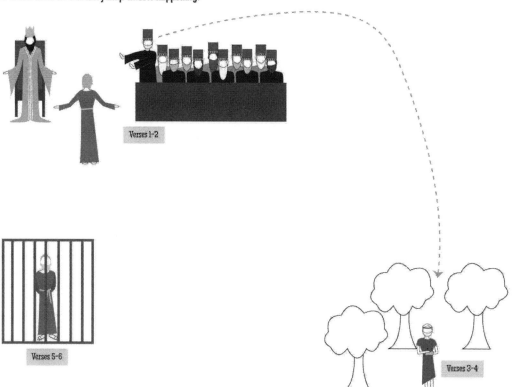

Verses 1-2

Verses 5-6

Verses 3-4

Why do we have the record of Abinadi's powerful words before King Noah and the council?	What can you learn from Alma and his character in this chapter?
Why did King Noah find Abinadi worthy of death? (verses 7-8)	What do you like about Abinadi's response? (verses 9-10)
What principles can you find in verse 11?	What principles can you find in verse 12?
What happens to Abinadi and what does he prophesy as he is being burned? (verses 13-18)	What principles can you find in verses 19-20?

ALMA IN THE WILDERNESS

MAKE A LIST OF THE EVENTS THAT HAPPENED IN VERSES 1-8 AND 14-16

1- ALMA REPENTED OF HIS SINS

OUR PART OF THE BAPTISMAL COVENANT	THE BAPTISMAL COVENANT	BAPTISM
8-9	10-13	14-16

THE CHURCH OF CHRIST	CHURCH ORGANIZATION	WHAT TO TEACH
17	18	19-20

COMMANDMENTS GIVEN	COMMANDMENTS GIVEN	COMMANDMENTS GIVEN
21-22	23-25	26-27

COMMANDMENTS GIVEN	ALMA'S PEOPLE	ALMA'S PEOPLE
28-29	30-31	32-35

MOSIAH 19 _____

Title for this chapter

IN EACH BOX, DRAW OR WRITE THE STORY IN THIS CHAPTER. ALSO INCLUDE DOCTRINES, PRINCIPLES, PERSONAL INSIGHTS AND LESSONS LEARNED.

KING NOAH'S ARMY IN SEARCH OF ALMA	DIVISION AMONG KING'S ARMY	GIDEON
1	2-3	4-5

GIDEON VS. KING NOAH / LAMANITES COMING	EVERYONE FLEES FROM LAMANITES	LAMANITES ATTACK
6-8	9	10

A KING'S DEVASTATING COMMAND	THOSE WHO DID NOT LEAVE / A TREATY	THE CONDITIONS
11	12-14	15

LIMHI	ALL BUT THE KING AND HIS PRIESTS	DEATH OF THE KING
16-17	18	19-21

A PROPHECY FULFILLED	REUNION	NEW KING, OATHS AND HEAVY TRIBUTE
(MOSIAH 12:3)	22-24	25-26

PEACE	GUARDS ALL AROUND	2 YEARS
27	28	29

MOSIAH 20

Title for this chapter

Study these verses and write on this story map what is happening. You could also draw more detail to add to the story.

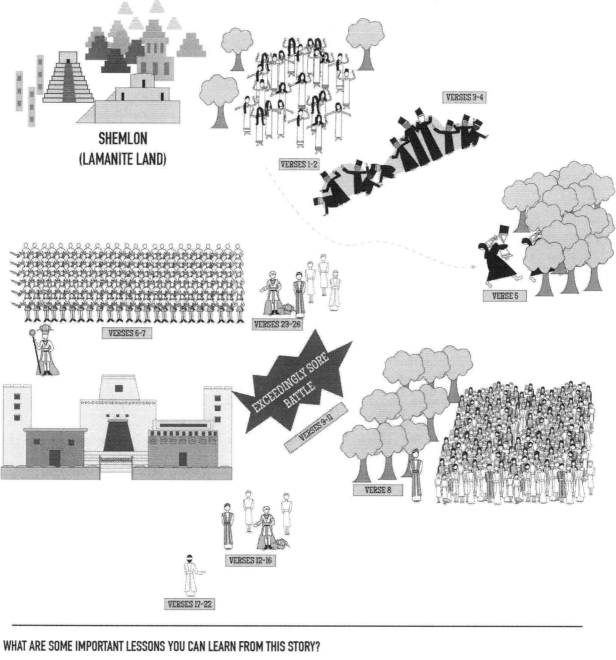

SHEMLON
(LAMANITE LAND)

VERSES 1-2

VERSES 3-4

VERSE 5

VERSES 6-7

VERSES 23-26

EXCEEDINGLY SORE BATTLE

VERSES 9-11

VERSE 8

VERSES 12-16

VERSES 17-22

WHAT ARE SOME IMPORTANT LESSONS YOU CAN LEARN FROM THIS STORY?

MOSIAH 21 _____

Title for this chapter

IN EACH BOX, DRAW OR WRITE THE STORY IN THIS CHAPTER. ALSO INCLUDE DOCTRINES, PRINCIPLES, PERSONAL INSIGHTS AND LESSONS LEARNED.

VERSES 1-2	VERSES 3-4	VERSE 5	VERSES 6-7
VERSES 8-10	VERSE 11	VERSE 12	VERSES 13-14
VERSES 15-16	VERSE 17	VERSE 18-19	VERSES 20-22

→ LOOK BACK AT MOSIAH 7. IN A FEW SENTENCES EXPLAIN WHO THESE PEOPLE ARE.

AMMON

KING LIMHI

Tip

After learning the history of Zeniff, Noah, and Limhi we are now at the same point in time as we were in Mosiah 7.

IN EACH BOX, CONTINUE TO DRAW OR WRITE THE STORY IN THIS CHAPTER. ALSO INCLUDE DOCTRINES, PRINCIPLES, PERSONAL INSIGHTS AND LESSONS LEARNED.

VERSES 23-24	VERSES 25-28	VERSE 29	VERSE 30	VERSE 31
VERSE 32	VERSE 33	VERSE 34	VERSE 35	VERSE 36

MOSIAH 22

In these boxes, doodle what you learn about Limhi, Ammon and the people escaping from the Land of Nephi. Write what is happening, draw pictures, make diagrams, write definitions, ask questions, record your insights.

1 Consulting with the people	The dilemma 2	Gideon 3-4	Gideon's Plan 5-8
9-10 The escape	The escape 11-12	Arrival to Zarahemla 13-14	Lamanites' Pursuit 15-16

Considering what you have learned in the past several chapters, what are some things you have learned from the following men?

AMMON

_____
_____
_____
_____
_____
_____
_____
_____
_____
_____
_____
_____

LIMHI

_____
_____
_____
_____
_____
_____
_____
_____
_____
_____
_____
_____

GIDEON

_____
_____
_____
_____
_____
_____
_____
_____
_____
_____
_____
_____

106

MOSIAH 23

Title for this chapter

In the last chapter Ammon was able to lead Limhi and his people to Zarahemla to reunite them with the rest of the Nephites. But there is still a group of Nephites who are out on their own! Alma and those that had followed him are still in the wilderness. Mosiah 23 and 24 jump back in time again as we learn what happened to this righteous group of Nephites once they had escaped King Noah's guards in Mosiah 18.

Study this chapter about Alma and the Nephites in the wilderness. In each box draw or write what is happening and doctrines and principles you find. Pay special attention to principles about how the Lord can be with us through various situations.

Verse 1	Verse 2	Verses 3–5	Verses 6–7

Verses 8–9	Verses 10–11	Verses 12–13	Verses 14–15

Verses 16–17	Verses 18–20	Verses 21–22	Verses 23–24

Verses 25–29	Verses 30–35	Verses 36–37	Verses 38–39

Study this chapter about Alma and the Nephites in the wilderness. In each box draw or write what is happening and doctrines and principles you find. Pay special attention to principles about how the Lord can be with us through various situations.

AMULON AND OTHER WICKED PRIESTS	THE KING OF THE LAMANITES	WHAT THEY TAUGHT THE PEOPLE	AMULON PERSECUTES ALMA & PEOPLE
Verses 1-2	Verse 3	Verses 4-7	Verses 8-9

ALMA & PEOPLE THREATENED	HOW ALMA & PEOPLE PRAYED	"THAT YE MAY STAND AS WITNESSES"	ALMA & PEOPLE STRENGTHENED
Verses 10-11	Verse 12	Verses 13-14	Verse 15

PROMISE OF DELIVERANCE	FAITH TO BE DELIVERED	DELIVERED	ARRIVAL IN ZARAHEMLA
Verses 16-17	Verse 18	Verses 19-22	Verses 23-25

What are some important life principles you learn from this chapter?

_____

_____

_____

_____

_____

_____

MOSIAH 25

Title for this chapter

KING MOSIAH II

MOSIAH GATHERS HIS PEOPLE VERSES 1-4

Study verses 1-4 and, in this space, record everything you learn about all of the people in Zarahemla. If you need a refresher on who the descendants of Mulek were, review page 82 in this journal.

Study this chapter and doodle, diagram, or record what is happening in each box. Include your personal thoughts and insights as you study the verses.

WHAT MOSIAH READ	THE PEOPLE'S REACTION TO WHAT MOSIAH READ	THE PEOPLE'S REACTION TO WHAT MOSIAH READ
VERSES 5-6	VERSE 7	VERSES 8-9
THE PEOPLE'S REACTION TO WHAT MOSIAH READ	**THE PEOPLE'S REACTION TO WHAT MOSIAH READ**	**THE CHILDREN OF AMULON**
VERSE 10	VERSE 11	VERSE 12
THE NEPHITES	**ALMA SPEAKS TO THE PEOPLE**	**LIMHI & HIS PEOPLE DESIRE TO BE BAPTIZED**
VERSE 13	VERSES 14-16	VERSES 17-18
ALMA ORGANIZES THE CHURCH	**ALMA ORGANIZES THE CHURCH**	**ALMA ORGANIZES THE CHURCH**
VERSE 19	VERSES 20-21	VERSES 22-24

LESSONS FROM ZARAHEMLA

WHAT VALUABLE LESSONS CAN YOU LEARN FROM THE PEOPLE IN ZARAHEMLA? WHAT CHRISTLIKE ATTRIBUTES HAVE YOU OBSERVED IN THEM, AND WHY ARE THEY IMPORTANT FOR US TO DEVELOP IN OUR OWN LIVES?

MOSIAH 26 _____

UNBELIEVING NEPHITES   Record what you learn about these Nephites in these verses 1-7.

ALMA'S RESPONSIBILITY   Record what you learn about Alma's responsibility and his concerns about this situation in verses 8-14.

THE LORD'S ANSWER   Study verses 15-32 and record important doctrines, principles, and phrases that the Lord told Alma.

ALMA'S RESPONSE   Record Alma's response in verses 33-34. What principles can you find in these verses?

THE RESULTS   Record what happened and what Alma did along with principles you find in verses 35-39.

MOSIAH 27 _____

es for this chapter

Study verses 1- 7. In the left box record the problem Alma and the members of the Church were facing.   In the right box record the solutions presented by King Mosiah.

THE PROBLEM	THE SOLUTION

Doodle what you learn about the Sons of Mosiah and one of the sons of Alma in verses 8-9.

Consider and then answer the following questions about these young men.

1. The Sons of Mosiah were the sons of the king of the Nephites. What kind of influence would they have because of who they were?

2. Alma the Younger was the Son of Alma. Alma (the elder) was the Prophet and founder of the church and had been through many things with King Noah, the Lamanites, and leading a group of Nephites back to Zarahemla. What kind of influence may Alma the Younger have had due to his father's position?

3. What particular skills did Alma the Younger have? (see verse 8)

4. What kind of impact was Alma the Younger having on the people? (see verse 9)

5. What do you think were some of the feelings and emotions King Mosiah and Alma experienced because of what these sons were doing?

112

IN EACH BOX, DRAW OR WRITE THE STORY THAT IS OCCURRING IN THESE VERSES IN MOSIAH 27. ALSO INCLUDE DOCTRINES, PRINCIPLES, PERSONAL INSIGHTS AND LESSONS LEARNED.

DESTROYING THE CHURCH OF GOD	THE ANGEL OF THE LORD	THE ANGEL OF THE LORD	THE ANGEL OF THE LORD
VERSE 10	VERSES 11-12	VERSE 13	VERSE 14
THE ANGEL OF THE LORD	**THE ANGEL OF THE LORD**	**IMPACT ON 5 YOUNG MEN**	**IMPACT ON ALMA**
VERSE 15	VERSES 16-17	VERSE 18	VERSE 19
TELLING ALMA (THE ELDER)	**ALMA GATHERS PEOPLE TO SEE**	**ALMA RECEIVES STRENGTH**	**ALMA TESTIFIES**
VERSE 20	VERSES 21-22	VERSE 23	VERSES 24-25
ALMA TESTIFIES	**ALMA TESTIFIES**	**ALMA TESTIFIES**	**ALMA AND SONS OF MOSIAH TRAVEL AND TEACH**
VERSES 26-27	VERSES 28-29	VERSES 30-31	VERSES 32-33
NAMES	**STRIVING TO REPAIR ALL INJURIES**	**INSTRUMENTS**	**HOW BLESSED ARE THEY!**
VERSE 34	VERSE 35	VERSE 36	VERSE 36

ALMA

LESSONS LEARNED
from
ALMA THE YOUNGER AND THE SONS OF MOSIAH

WHAT VALUABLE LESSONS CAN YOU LEARN FROM THE STORY OF THESE FIVE YOUNG MEN?

_____
_____
_____
_____
_____
_____
_____
_____
_____
_____
_____
_____
_____
_____
_____
_____
_____
_____
_____
_____
_____
_____
_____
_____
_____
_____
_____
_____
_____
_____
_____
_____
_____

MOSIAH 28 _____

VERSES 1-5

WHAT DO YOU LEARN ABOUT THE SONS OF MOSIAH AND THEIR DESIRES IN THESE VERSES?

VERSES 6-8

WHAT DO YOU LEARN ABOUT KING MOSIAH AND THE ANSWER HE RECEIVED FROM THE LORD IN THESE VERSES? *CONSIDER THE DANGEROUS REQUEST THESE SONS HAD ASKED OF THEIR FATHER.

DRAW, DOODLE, DIAGRAM, OR WRITE WHAT IS HAPPENING IN THE FOLLOWING VERSES.

VERSES 9-10	VERSES 11-12
VERSES 13-16 * THESE THINGS = THE TWO STONES	**VERSES 17-18**
VERSE 19 * THIS ACCOUNT = THE BOOK OF ETHER	**VERSE 20**

MOSIAH 29

Title for this chapter

DRAW, DOODLE, OR RECORD WHAT IS HAPPENING AND WHAT YOU LEARN IN THE FOLLOWING VERSES.

NEXT NEPHITE KING	ANNOUNCEMENT TO PEOPLE	ISSUES MOSIAH FORESEES	FROM KINGS TO JUDGES
VERSES 1-3	VERSES 4-6	VERSES 7-9	VERSES 10-11

THE IDEAL JUDGE	IF IT WERE POSSIBLE...	THE INFLUENCE OF A WICKED KING	REMEMBER KING NOAH
VERSE 12	VERSES 13-15	VERSES 16-17	VERSES 18-20

DETHRONING A WICKED KING	A WICKED KING'S LAWS	CHOOSE JUDGES	THE VOICE OF THE PEOPLE
VERSES 21-22	VERSE 23	VERSES 24-25	VERSES 26-27

JUDGING THE JUDGES	JUDGING THE JUDGES	AVOIDING INIQUITY CAUSED BY KINGS	A LAND OF LIBERTY
VERSE 28	VERSE 29	VERSES 30-31	VERSE 32

THAT EVERY MAN MIGHT BEAR HIS PART	DISADVANTAGES OF AN UNRIGHTEOUS KING	PEOPLE DESIRE TO NOT HAVE KINGS	A LAND OF LIBERTY
VERSE 33-34	VERSE 35-36	VERSES 37-38	VERSE 39

LOVE FOR MOSIAH	JUDGES APPOINTED	ALMA CHIEF JUDGE & HIGH PRIEST	ALMA THE ELDER & MOSIAH DIE
VERSE 40	VERSE 41	VERSES 42-44	VERSES 45-47

MY COMMENTARY

As you are studying the Book of Mormon and have thoughts you would like to record, use these pages to record your valuable insights. Use the left column to record the page and scripture you were studying and are now writing about. You may only write a few sentences or you may write several pages of your own commentary. After you have finished writing, go back to the pages you were originally studying and make a note on the bottom of the page that you have written commentary in the back of this book. For example you may write: "My commentary on page 118".

SCRIPTURE/
PAGE

MY COMMENTARY

MY COMMENTARY

MY COMMENTARY

MY COMMENTARY

MY COMMENTARY

MY COMMENTARY

MY COMMENTARY

MY COMMENTARY

MY COMMENTARY

MY COMMENTARY

SCRIPTURE/
PAGE

MY COMMENTARY

MY COMMENTARY

MY COMMENTARY

MY COMMENTARY

MY COMMENTARY

MY COMMENTARY

MY COMMENTARY

MY COMMENTARY

MY COMMENTARY

MY COMMENTARY

MY COMMENTARY

MY COMMENTARY

MY COMMENTARY

MY COMMENTARY

MY COMMENTARY

MY COMMENTARY

MY COMMENTARY

MY COMMENTARY

MY COMMENTARY

MY COMMENTARY

MY COMMENTARY

MY COMMENTARY

MY COMMENTARY

MY COMMENTARY

MY COMMENTARY

MY COMMENTARY

MY COMMENTARY

MY COMMENTARY

MY COMMENTARY

MY COMMENTARY

MY COMMENTARY

MY COMMENTARY

Made in the USA
San Bernardino, CA
03 March 2016